IMAGES OF WAR

ALLIED ARMOURED FIGHTING VEHICLES OF THE SECOND WORLD WAR

RARE PHOTOGRAPHS FROM WARTIME ARCHIVES

Michael Green

Pen & Sword
MILITARY

First published in Great Britain in 2017 by
PEN & SWORD MILITARY
An imprint of
Pen & Sword Books Ltd
47 Church Street
Barnsley
South Yorkshire
S70 2AS

ISBN 978-1-47387-237-0

Typeset by Concept, Huddersfield, West Yorkshire HD4 5JL.
Printed and bound in India by Replika Press Pvt. Ltd.

Pen & Sword Books Ltd incorporates the imprints of Pen & Sword Archaeology, Atlas, Aviation, Battleground, Discovery, Family History, History, Maritime, Military, Naval, Politics, Railways, Select, Social History, Transport, True Crime, and Claymore Press, Frontline Books, Leo Cooper, Praetorian Press, Remember When, Seaforth Publishing and Wharncliffe.

For a complete list of Pen & Sword titles please contact
PEN & SWORD BOOKS LIMITED
47 Church Street, Barnsley, South Yorkshire S70 2AS, England
E-mail: enquiries@pen-and-sword.co.uk
Website: www.pen-and-sword.co.uk

Contents

Dedication

The author would like to dedicate this book to Philip M. Cavanaugh,
a former director of the now-closed Patton Museum of Armor and Cavalry
who was always most helpful during the author's research visits to the facility.

Foreword

In his latest work, *Allied Armoured Fighting Vehicles of the Second World War*, author Michael Green continues his previous work on *Allied Tanks of the Second World War*, making this a fine companion volume. This work fits well into the historiography of the Second World War and the weapons systems employed in that war. Green discusses the vast array of armoured fighting vehicles developed by the Allies both before and during the worldwide struggle.

The strong emphasis on American-designed and built armoured fighting vehicles in this work reflects the country's unmatched industrial output during the conflict. This came about because the American automobile industry offered its services to build all the military vehicles required by our own armed forces as well as those of the Allies. This was a war-winning arrangement as it had the necessary experience of mass-producing vehicles, a trained workforce and the facilities needed for assembly-line production.

Visually stunning with many rare photos from archives around the world, Green shows us the tank destroyers, self-propelled artillery, armoured cars, half-tracks and gun motor carriages that helped the Allied armies prevail over those of the Axis powers. Following a layout and writing style that is familiar to readers, Green once again gets to the core of armoured fighting vehicle design, both successful and failed designs.

Randy R. Talbot
Command Historian (retired)
US Army TACOM Life Cycle Management Command

Acknowledgments

As with any published work, authors must depend on a great many people for assistance. These included, over many years, my fellow author and long-time mentor the late Richard Hunnicutt. Other friends who kindly supplied information and pictures for this work are credited in the captions.

Both the paid and volunteer staff of the now-closed Patton Museum of Cavalry and Armor provided the author with a great deal of assistance over many years. For the sake of brevity all images from the former Patton Museum of Cavalry and Armor will be credited to the 'Patton Museum'.

I am also indebted to David Fletcher, fellow author and the long-time former librarian at the Tank Museum located in Bovington, England. He has greatly assisted the author in locating photographs for many of his books, including this one. All images from the Tank Museum will be credited to just 'Tank Museum' for brevity.

A US army entity that assisted the author in acquiring historical photographs of American tanks for this work was the Command Historian's Office of the TACOM Life Cycle Management Command (LCMC). All pictures from this organization are credited to 'TACOM', again for the sake of brevity.

Chapter One

Reconnaissance Vehicles

The armoured car had its baptism of fire in 1912 during the Italian-Turkish War (1911–12). This was four years before the first tank entered into combat during the First World War (1914–18). Beside their employment as raiding vehicles or rescuing downed pilots behind enemy lines, armoured cars also saw limited service as reconnaissance vehicles during the early part of the First World War. The latter would become their primary role during the Second World War.

In the British and Commonwealth armies, the armoured car was the ground reconnaissance platform of choice during the Second World War. The Red Army originally favoured light tanks for its reconnaissance role but eventually decided that the cheaper and quicker-to-build armoured cars made more sense. The US army would field an armoured car during the Second World War but seemed to prefer light tanks for scouting purposes. Some armies also employed armoured half-tracks in the reconnaissance role for a time.

Early British Armoured Cars

The first post-First World War armoured car adopted by the British army in 1927 was the 6 × 4 Crossley Mark I. It was built upon a specially-designed Crossley Motors truck chassis. Weighing in at approximately 11,000lb it had a four-man crew and was armed only with machine guns. The Crossley Mark I was employed only as a training vehicle by the British army during the early part of the Second World War.

The first purpose-built armoured car acquired by the British army in 1928 was named the 'Lanchester' after the firm that designed and built the vehicle. A 6 × 4 vehicle with a crew of four, it was armed only with machine guns. In its final version the vehicle weighed approximately 16,000lb. There were thirty-nine units built. Some were sent to the Far East in 1939, with a few seeing combat against the Japanese army in 1941.

Second-Life Armoured Cars

The Royal Navy Air Service had employed improvised machine-gun-armed 4 × 4 Rolls-Royce armoured cars in 1914 to rescue pilots forced down behind enemy lines during the First World War. However, once both sides had dug in and trench-fighting became more common, this was no longer possible. These approximately 9,000lb vehicles labelled as the '1914 Pattern' were then transferred to the British army in 1915 who found limited use for them during the remainder of the conflict due to all sides building extensive trench systems.

Some new-built examples of the Rolls-Royce armoured cars appeared during the interwar period and are referred to as the '1920 Pattern' or '1924 Pattern'. A number of 1914 Pattern armoured cars were rebuilt during the interwar period. Besides the British army, these Rolls-Royce armoured cars were also employed by the Armoured Car companies of the Royal Air Force (RAF), being tasked with airfield defence.

A number of the Rolls-Royce armoured cars would remain in service long enough to see combat in the Middle East during the early part of the Second World War. These were employed by both the British army and the Armoured Car companies of the RAF, which became the RAF Regiment in 1942. Others were retained in Great Britain and employed as training vehicles. They were officially labelled as a 'Light Reconnaissance Car'.

In the early 1920s, the British army in India was supplied with approximately 100 machine-gun-armed armoured cars based on a Crossley 4 × 4 commercial truck chassis. Labelled as the 'Crossley India Pattern', they rode on solid rubber tyres. In 1939, many had their armoured bodywork removed and remounted on a 4 × 4 Chevrolet truck chassis that rode on pneumatic tyres. They were renamed as the 'Crossley Chevrolet India Pattern' and some saw service in the Middle East between 1940 and 1941.

The Beaverettes

With the fall of France in the summer of 1940 there loomed the threat of German paratroopers attacking British airfields and aircraft factories. In response, a senior British politician (Lord Beaverbrook) arranged for the construction of a stopgap armoured vehicle built upon the chassis of an existing 4 × 2 civilian car and armed with machine guns.

Its official British army designation was the Standard Car 4 × 2 or Car Armoured Light Standard. The RAF labelled it the Car, Armoured, Light Standard Type C Beaverette I. The approximately 5,000lb so-called Beaverettes were operated by a crew of two. In total, there were around 2,800 units built in different versions.

The initial version of the Beaverette was open-topped but subsequent models had an armoured roof and were fitted with a small one-man turret. Some were allocated to British army units as interim reconnaissance vehicles until more capable vehicles were acquired. None would leave the country to see combat.

The Humberettes

Another stopgap armoured vehicle pressed into service in the summer of 1940 was the Humber Light Reconnaissance Car Mark I. It was officially named 'Ironside I' after British General Sir Edmund Ironside who had authorized their construction. It also acquired the unofficial nickname 'Humberette'.

The Humber Light Reconnaissance Car was originally based on the 4 × 2 chassis of the 'Super Snipe' passenger car. The three-man Mark I model weighed approximately 7,000lb and had an armoured roof. The Mark II version came with a one-man open-topped turret armed with a machine gun. It could also be armed with the Rifle, Anti-tank, .55 Boys, better known as the 'Boys Anti-tank Rifle'.

Beginning with the approximately 8,000lb Mark III version, the Humber Light Reconnaissance Car became a 4 × 4 vehicle. It was the Mark III variant that became the main operational version for the British army. These would see service almost everywhere that the British military fought during the Second World War. By the time production concluded in 1943, a total of 3,599 units had been constructed.

General Motors of Canada built 1,761 units of a near-copy of the Humber Light Reconnaissance Car named the 'Otter'. Its official designation was 'Car, Light Reconnaissance, Canadian GM Mark I'. Most served with the Canadian army. However, some of the approximately 11,000lb vehicles would be taken into service by the British army.

The Morris Contribution

In 1938 the British army ordered somewhere between 100 and 120 production units of the Morris Armoured Reconnaissance Car Model CS9. It was based on a lengthened chassis of a Morris Motors Ltd 4 × 4 truck chassis and had a four-man crew with two positioned in an open-topped turret armed with a machine gun and a Boys Anti-tank Rifle. The approximately 10,000lb vehicle would see combat in both France and later in North Africa until withdrawn from service in 1941.

Morris Motors Ltd came up with the Mark I Light Reconnaissance Car in 1942. Like the others, it was based on the chassis of a 4 × 2 civilian car but differed in overall design as the engine was moved to the rear of the vehicle. It was operated by up to three men and armed with a machine gun and the .55 Boys Anti-tank Rifle. The total number taken into service was 1,914 units.

The Mark II version of the Morris Light Reconnaissance Car was a 4 × 4 vehicle. It was armed only with a machine gun as the Boys Anti-tank Rifle that had been fitted to the Mark I was then considered obsolete. A total of 2,274 units of this vehicle were built between the summer of 1940 and 1944. It would see service with the British army from North Africa to Western Europe and would also serve with the RAF Regiment.

The Dingo and Variants

The Daimler Scout Car unofficially nicknamed the 'Dingo' entered into British army service in 1940 with the requirements for the vehicle having been set down in 1938. It was a turretless two-man vehicle armed with a machine gun. The original model had a sliding roof dispensed with on later versions.

The Daimler Scout Car was a purpose-built design and therefore had excellent off-road capabilities. The total number constructed of the three versions of the vehicle was 6,626 units. Besides its use as a reconnaissance vehicle, the approximately 7,000lb scout car was also employed as a non-combat liaison vehicle.

As Daimler could not build as many scout cars as the British and Commonwealth armies required, other firms both inside and outside the country were tasked with designing and building similar vehicles. The Ford Motor Company of Canada built 3,255 units of a larger and heavier version of the Dingo named the 'Lynx'. It weighed approximately 9,000lb and came in two models officially labelled as the 'Car Scout Ford I and II'.

Whereas the Ford-built Lynx series looked very much like the Daimler-built scout car series and can be difficult to distinguish, a machine-gun-armed scout car designed and built by Humber Limited, a subsidiary of the Rootes Group, looked very different and is easily identified by its unique design.

Like the Daimler and Ford vehicles, the Humber Scout Car was a rear-engine vehicle with a crew of two at the front of the vehicle. It weighed around 5,000lb and between 1942 and 1945 a total of 4,102 units were built in two versions. Not as capable as the Daimler Scout Car, the Humber Scout Car series was generally reserved for the non-combat liaison role.

Daimler Armoured Car

The Daimler Scout Car and its machine-gun-armed counterparts were intended to acquire battlefield information by stealth. This led to the demand for a better-armed version that could better defend itself when the need arose. This resulted in the fielding of the Daimler Armoured Car Mark I in 1941 and later the Daimler Armoured Car Mark II, beginning in 1944.

The Daimler Armoured Car was an up-scaled Daimler Scout Car fitted with a two-man tank turret armed with the Ordnance, QF (Quick-Firing), 2-pounder (40mm) gun and a machine gun. The vehicle weighed approximately 17,000lb. A total of 2,318 units of the Daimler Armoured Car series were built, 1,900 of these being the Mark I model and 418 being the Mark II variant.

Guy/Humber Armoured Cars

In 1939, Guy Motors was awarded a contract to build 101 units of a machine-gun-armed armoured car designated the Mark I. It was based on the chassis of a 4 × 4 artillery prime mover and weighed approximately 13,000lb. A few would see combat with the British army during the Battle for France.

As Guy Motors could not meet all the requirements of the British army, it was decided that Humber Limited would be assigned the job of designing and building a similar armoured car. Like Guy Motors, they decided to use the chassis of a 4 × 4 artillery prime mover upon which they mounted an armoured hull and turret very similar to that seen on the Guy Armoured Car Mark I. The Humber Armoured Car Mark I began coming off the production line in 1940.

The Humber Armoured Car Mark I weighed approximately 15,000lb. The last production model of the series was the Mark IV. It was armed with the American-built 37mm Gun M6 plus machine guns. Total production of all variants of the vehicle was 2,000 units. The Daimler Armoured Car Mark I was the intended replacement for the Humber Armoured Car series.

To supplement the Humber Armoured Car series built in Great Britain, General Motors of Canada came up with their own copy they labelled as the 'Fox Mark I'. A total of 1,506 units of the vehicle were built beginning in 1942 and saw widespread use with Commonwealth forces.

Late-War Armoured Car

The planned replacement for both the Daimler and Humber armoured cars was the Coventry Mark I Armoured Car that appeared in 1944. Its design and construction were a combined effort of the firms of both Daimler and Humber, although in its final form it resembled the Daimler Armoured Car series rather than any of the Humber Armoured Car series.

The armament on the Coventry Mark I Armoured Car consisted of a 2-pounder cannon and a machine gun. Considered obsolete by the time it went into production, only 220 units were completed before the Second World War ended. None would see combat with the British or Commonwealth armies.

AEC Heavy Armoured Car

Perceiving a need by the British army for a much better-armed and armoured car than existed in 1941, the Associated Equipment Company Limited (AEC) as a private venture designed and built a 4 × 4 prototype armoured car on the chassis of a commercial truck. It was fitted with a tank turret armed with a 2-pounder cannon in addition to machine guns. The British army was impressed with what they saw and ordered the AEC Heavy Armoured Car series into production.

The Mark I model of the AEC Heavy Armoured Car series was a near copy of the prototype, with 129 units built. The Mark II model was armed with a turret-mounted Ordnance, QF, 6-pounder (57mm) gun plus machine guns. The Mark III model was armed with the turret-mounted Ordnance, QF, 75mm gun plus machine guns. In total, 200 units of the AEC Heavy Armoured Car series were constructed between 1942 and 1943.

South African Armoured Cars

Upon the start of the Second World War, South Africa (then referred to as the Union of South Africa) decided to build its own armoured cars, which they designated as armoured reconnaissance cars. A locally-produced Ford Motors of Canada 4 × 2 commercial truck chassis was chosen, upon which an armoured hull and turret were fitted. Armament would originally consist only of a single machine gun for the first two versions of the vehicle labelled the Mark I and II.

The approximately 13,000lb Mark II model of the South African armoured reconnaissance car as well as all subsequent versions up through to the 14,000lb Mark IV were upgraded to a 4 × 4 configuration by the addition of conversion kits supplied by the American firm of Marmon-Herrington. This resulted in the Mark II through to Mark IV armoured reconnaissance cars being referred to as the 'Marmon-Herringtons'.

The Mark II and Mark III versions of the South African armoured reconnaissance cars were armed with a machine gun and a Boys Anti-tank Rifle. The Mark IV version was completely redesigned and incorporated all the lessons learned from the previous three models. It had a new larger turret armed with a 2-pounder cannon plus machine guns. In total, 5,746 units of the South African-built armoured reconnaissance car series were constructed by 1944.

Indian and Australian Armoured Cars

In 1939, Indian industry took it upon itself to design and build its own armoured car. It was decided to use a Ford Motors of Canada 4 × 2 commercial truck chassis later upgraded into a 4 × 4 vehicle. The first two models of what became known as the 'Indian Pattern Carrier' were turretless and armed only with a machine gun. Later models had a machine-gun-armed open-topped turret. A total of 4,655 units were built between 1940 and 1944 of the approximately 6,000lb vehicle.

Australian industry, like its Commonwealth counterparts, also decided to design and build its own armoured cars in the early part of the Second World War. This resulted in the Australian army taking into service two improvised armoured cars. Both were based on the modified chassis of trucks built by the Ford Motor Company of Australia and fitted with locally-made armoured hulls.

The Australian army vehicles were the Light Armoured Car Mark I and Mark II models, both named the 'Rover'. There were also the Mark I and Mark II versions of a scout car named the 'Dingo'. There were less than 100 built of the Rover models and a combined total of 245 units constructed of the Dingo. Neither would see service outside their home country due to numerous design limitations.

The Universal Carrier

In 1936 the British firm of Vickers-Armstrong came up with the prototype of a small full-tracked armoured vehicle with an open top. The following year a revised version was ordered into production as the Carrier, Machine Gun, Number 2, Mark I. Reflecting one of the two types of machine gun with which it was fitted, the vehicle was unofficially nicknamed the 'Bren Gun Carrier'.

There appeared other specialized versions of the Bren Gun Carrier series in British army service prior to the Second World War. These included the Carrier, Scout, Mark I and the Carrier, Cavalry, Mark I. In April 1939, the British army decided that it made more sense to have only a single version of the Bren Gun Carrier built and labelled it as the 'Universal Carrier', which could then be configured to serve in different roles. It weighed approximately 9,000lb.

To meet British and Commonwealth army requirements, the Universal Carrier was built in a number of different countries. Besides the approximately 35,000 units built in Great Britain, roughly another 29,000 units were built in Canada. Australian industry contributed about 5,000 units, with another 600 built in New Zealand. Approximately 20,000 units of an enlarged and redesigned variant built in the United States received the designation Universal Carrier T16. However, the US army did not adopt the 10,500lb T16.

American Armoured Cars for the British Army

British industry proved unable to meet the needs of its armed forces in 1940 for a suitable number of larger armoured cars armed with high-velocity anti-tank guns. The British government therefore wanted to pay American industry to build British-designed armoured cars. This request was denied by the American government. Only

American-designed armoured cars acceptable to the US army could be ordered and paid for by the British government.

The US army also saw a requirement for medium and heavy armoured cars in 1940. This resulted in a number of projects being authorized for development by American industry. As events transpired, only a single 4 × 4 General Motors-designed medium armoured car entered into large-scale production. It was designated as the T17E1. In anticipation of it being taken into service, the US army designated it as the Armored Car Medium M6.

In December 1942, the US army re-evaluated its requirements for medium and heavy armoured cars and decided that they were not needed as they weighed too much. However, the British and Commonwealth armies remained interested in the T17E1 and permission was granted by the United States government for American industry to build them for Lend-Lease, beginning in March 1941.

A total of 2,844 units of the T17E1 were therefore built between 1942 and 1943. The British army named it the 'Staghound'. The approximately 31,000lb vehicle was armed with the 37mm Gun M6 and machine guns. There was a small number constructed of an improvised version fitted with a tank turret armed with a 75mm main gun labelled as the Staghound Mark III. In Australian army service the T17E1 was designated as the Car, Armoured, Heavy, and nicknamed the 'Stag'.

Failed Medium and Heavy Armoured Cars

In a similar scenario to the General Motors Staghound armoured car, Ford Motors designed and built a 6 × 6 medium armoured car designated the T17. When the US army decided it did not want the approximately 28,000lb vehicle, it was approved for production to meet British and Commonwealth army requirements. The British army went ahead and named the T17 as the 'Deerhound' but later rejected it. Of the 250 units built, most had their 37mm M6 guns removed and were assigned to US army military police units based in the United States.

In 1940, it was envisioned that there would be a requirement for a heavy armoured car by both the US and British armies. This led to the development and testing of a General Motors-designed and built 8 × 8 heavy armoured car designated as the T18. It was originally to be armed with the 37mm Gun M6. However, by the time the pilot vehicle was ready for testing in July 1942 it was clear that its main armament was obsolete.

The rejection of the 37mm Gun M6 on the T18 led to arming a second pilot of the vehicle with the 57mm Gun M1 and a new designation as the T18E2. By this time the US army had lost interest but the British army still wanted 2,500 units of the approximately 53,000lb vehicle, which they went ahead and named 'Boarhound'. However, British army interest in the vehicle soon waned and eventually only thirty units were built before the programme was cancelled.

French Army Reconnaissance Vehicles

The French army was plagued by funding shortfalls before the Second World War. This meant that their efforts to modernize their armoured fighting vehicle inventory were incomplete when the Germans invaded. The oldest armoured car in service would be 100 units of an upgraded First World War-era armoured car labelled as the AMD Laffly 50 AM. Of that number, only twenty were in France when the Germans invaded, with the other eighty vehicles serving overseas in French colonies.

The four-man AMD Laffly 50 AM weighed approximately 13,000lb. It was armed with a 37mm main gun with a machine gun being added in 1931. Its intended replacement was to be an upgraded model referred to as the Laffly 80 AM. By the time the first examples left the factory floor in 1935, the French army had grasped the fact that it was already obsolete and capped production at only twenty-eight units.

The 4 × 2 AMD Laffly 50 AM and the 4 × 2 Laffly 80 AM would serve alongside 100 units of a three-man reconnaissance half-track designated as the AMC Schneider

P 16. There were also fifty units of another reconnaissance half-track labelled as the AMC Citroen P 28 built in the 1930s. Both were armed with 37mm main guns and had machine guns. Both were considered failures in service by the French army with the AMC Citroen P 28 being pulled from the inventory before the German invasion.

The most modern armoured car in service with the French army in 1940 was the four-man Panhard AMD 35, also commonly referred to as the Panhard Type 178. Introduced into service in 1937, the four-man purpose-built vehicle weighed approximately 19,000lb and was armed with the 25mm SA35 gun. There were 370 units of the Panhard Type 178 in service when the Germans invaded. The German army thought enough of the vehicle to impress it into service following the fall of France.

Red Army Armoured Cars

In 1936 the Red Army began fielding a light armoured car designated the BA-20. It was the replacement for the FAI light armored car that had entered service in 1933. The three-man BA-20 was armed with a single machine gun and weighed approximately 6,000lb. To complement the BA-20 series the Red Army would take into service a series of heavy armoured cars. The Red Army defined a heavy car as one armed with a cannon, while light armoured cars were armed only with machine guns.

The first mass-produced medium armoured car was the BAI armed with the 37mm Hotchkiss gun (PS-1) and a machine gun. As the BAI proved under-armed and overweight it was replaced in 1934 by the improved BA-3 armed with the 45mm gun 20K (mod. 1932) and a machine gun. It weighed approximately 15,000lb. The BA-3 was eventually replaced on the production line in 1936 by the very similar-looking BA-6 that weighed approximately 13,000lb. A total of 394 units of the BA-3 were built and 386 units of the BA-6.

An up-armoured variant of the BA-6 with a redesigned turret was labelled as the B-10A and appeared in 1938. An improved version that entered into production in 1939 was labelled as the BA-10M. Total production of the BA-10 series between 1938 and 1941 amounted to 3,331 units. With the German invasion of the Soviet Union in the summer of 1941, the Red Army halted the production of all armoured cars in favour of tank production.

It was not until early 1942 that the Red Army authorized production of a new light armoured car designated as the BA-64. Armed only with a machine gun, the two-man vehicle weighed approximately 6,000lb. There were two versions of the vehicle: the original BA-64, of which 3,903 units were constructed, and an improved model labelled the BA-64B with 5,160 units built.

Early US Army Reconnaissance Vehicles

The US army explored a number of possible candidate vehicles for the reconnaissance role beginning in the late 1920s. In 1934 they accepted for service the machine-gun-armed 6 × 4 Armoured Car M1. The four-man vehicle weighed approximately 11,000lb. Not counting two prototypes, only twelve units of the M1 Armoured Car were built between 1934 and 1938 by James Cunningham, Son & Co.

Between 1935 and 1937 the US army took into service seventy-three units of the 4 × 4 M1 Scout Car built by the White Motor Company. The vehicle was open-topped and based on the chassis of a 4 × 4 commercial truck. The machine guns of the M1 Scout Car were attached to fixed mounts located inside the vehicle as well as on the outside. The approximately 8,000lb vehicle had a top speed of 50mph.

The M1 Scout Car was quickly followed on the White production line in 1937 by another very similar-looking vehicle referred to as the M2 Scout Car. A total of twenty-two units of the vehicle were built between 1935 and 1938, with 100 units of an improved version originally labelled as the M2A1 Scout Car and later redesignated as the M3 Scout Car also being built between 1936 and 1939.

In 1939 a progressively-improved version of the M3 Scout Car came off the White production lines and was designated as the M3A1. It was open-topped and armed only with machine guns. Between 1939 and 1944 20,894 units of the M3A1 Scout Car were built.

Lend-Lease Scout Cars

A total of 11,400 units of the approximately 9,000lb M3A1 Scout Car were allocated to Lend-Lease, with the majority going to the British army and most of the rest being supplied to the Red Army. In British army service the vehicle was unofficially nick-named the 'White' after the American company that built them.

The M3A1 Scout Car was generally regarded by the British army as an armoured truck rather than a reconnaissance vehicle. This is reflected in its original designation as a scout car being later changed to the 'Truck, 15cwt, 4 × 4, Armoured Personnel' by the British army. The Red Army used them for everything from command vehicles to towing anti-tank guns.

Replacing the M3A1 Scout Car

The M3A1 Scout Car proved to be a major disappointment for the US army due to its poor off-road performance. With no suitable wheeled reconnaissance vehicle yet in production other than the non-armoured 4 × 4 vehicles, the US army was forced in late 1940 to employ machine-gun-armed half-tracks as interim reconnaissance vehicles.

The armoured half-tracks pushed into the reconnaissance role would include the multi-purpose M2 Half-Track Car and the larger M3 Half-Track Personnel Carrier. Due to the large number of such vehicles ordered by the US army in 1940 and 1941, their production was farmed out to two other firms besides White.

In the British and Commonwealth armies the various types of American-supplied armoured half-tracks were sometimes employed by the assault troops of Reconnaissance Regiments (Recce Regiments) instead of unarmoured trucks. Reconnaissance Regiments were attached to British and Commonwealth infantry divisions.

A New Armoured Car

The US army's replacement for armoured half-tracks in the reconnaissance role proved to be the Ford-designed and built 6 × 6 M8 Light Armoured Car, which entered into production in 1942. Originally envisioned as a tank destroyer, by the time it entered production its 37mm Gun M6 was not up to the task of destroying enemy tanks. Besides its main gun, the four-man M8 was also armed with two machine guns.

With the approximately 17,000lb M8 being unable to fulfil its original role as a tank destroyer, it was then seen as a suitable replacement for the M3A1 Scout Car. As it was designed with standard truck-type suspension components in order to keep costs down and speed up production, the M8 had very poor off-road performance. The vehicle's open-topped turret also left the crew highly vulnerable to enemy grenades as well as mortar and artillery fragments.

Production of the M8 would continue until 1945, with a total of 8,523 units constructed. Some were supplied to the British army under Lend-Lease and saw limited use in Italy. The British army named them the 'Greyhound'. There were also 3,791 units built of a non-turreted version of the M8 labelled the M20 Armoured Utility Vehicle. Sometimes armed with a machine gun, the primary role of the M20 was as a non-combat liaison vehicle.

Possible Replacements

The poor off-road mobility of the M8 Light Armoured Car resulted in the development and testing of two light armoured cars labelled the T27 and T28. Both were fitted with independently-sprung suspension systems and therefore had superior off-road mobility compared to the M8. Of the two, the US army decided the approximately 15,000lb 6 × 6 T28, later redesignated as the M38, was the better choice. However, the war ended before it was placed into production and it was soon cancelled.

In January 1944, the US army decided to test the concept of turretless light tanks being employed as command or reconnaissance vehicles. This had been something the British army had pioneered during the North African campaign using American Lend-Lease-supplied Light Tank M3s. By the time the US army began exploring the idea, the Light Tank M3 had already been replaced in service by the Light Tank M5A1.

The US army had two slightly different turretless pilot examples of the Light Tank M5A1 reconfigured and labelled the Full-Track Reconnaissance Vehicles T8 and T8E1. Their off-road mobility was far superior to the Light Armoured Car M8 but the US army felt that they were under-armed with only a single large-calibre machine gun. At that point in time it was decided that the Light Tank M24 armed with a 75mm main gun was far more suitable as a reconnaissance vehicle and neither the T8 nor T8E1 was placed into production.

Pictured is an interwar Crossley Motors 6 × 4 experimental armoured car built for consideration by the British military. It is fitted with the machine-gun-armed turret from a British army light tank. The model eventually selected by the British military in the late 1920s looked very much the same but was armed with a machine-gun-armed turret from a later model British light tank. (*Tank Museum*)

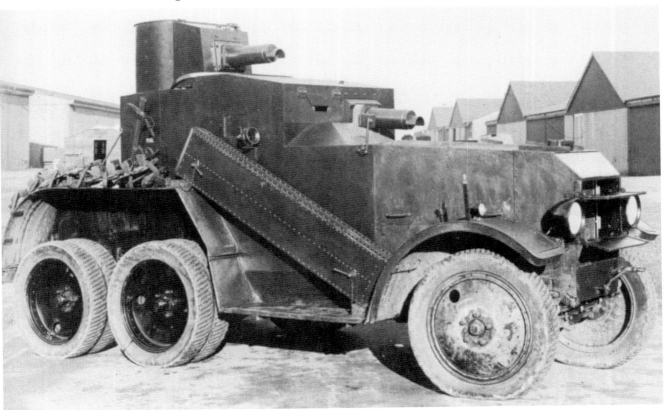

(*Opposite above*) A preserved example of a Lanchester Mark II Armoured Car armed with both a turret-mounted and a front hull-mounted water-cooled machine gun. The vehicle has a maximum armour thickness of 10mm. It is 20ft in length, has a width of 6ft 7.5in and a height of 9ft 3in. The gasoline-powered engine gave it a top speed on level roads of 45mph. (*Tank Museum*)

(*Above*) Pictured is a restored Pattern 1920 Rolls-Royce Armoured Car. The wire-spoked rims of the original First World War-era Pattern 1914 model have been dispensed with and replaced by more modern solid wheel hubs. The vehicle's main armament remains as it had been in the First World War: a single water-cooled machine gun. Maximum armour thickness was only 8mm. (*Ian Wilcox*)

(*Opposite below*) Photographed in North Africa are two Fordson armoured cars belonging to one of the RAF Armoured Car Companies. These were improvised vehicles in which the armoured hulls and turrets of mechanically worn-out Rolls-Royce armoured cars were re-mounted on a modern 4 × 2 truck chassis built by Fordson, the United Kingdom branch of the Ford Motor Company. (*Tank Museum*)

During the interwar period some British army units in India were equipped with the 4 × 4 Crossley Armoured Car, India Pattern as seen here. It had a non-rotating dome-shaped turret for the fitting of two machine guns. Some of these vehicles would later have their turrets and hulls transferred to a more modern General Motors truck chassis and would see action early in the Second World War. *(Author's collection)*

On museum display is a British military armoured car labelled the Beaverette Mark III and also nicknamed the 'Beaverbug'. It was the final model in a line of improvised armoured cars built upon the chassis of 4 × 2 civilian cars following the fall of France and the fear of a German invasion of England in 1940. They were employed by both the British army and the Armoured Car Companies of the Royal Air Force. *(Tank Museum)*

Two 4 × 4 Humber Light Reconnaissance Car Mark IIIs are shown in Western Europe during the Second World War. The roundels on the vehicles' hulls identify them as belonging to the RAF Regiment formed in 1942 out of the former RAF Armoured Car Companies. The American military stars on the vehicles were intended to prevent friendly-fire incidents. (*Tank Museum*)

In this museum diorama is a restored example of a 4 × 4 Humber Light Reconnaissance Car Mark III in British army markings. The vehicle has a length of 14ft 4in, a width of 6ft 2in and a height of 7ft 1in. The maximum armour thickness on the vehicle is 10mm and it had a top road speed of 60mph. (*Ian Wilcox*)

To supplement British production of the 4 × 4 Humber Light Reconnaissance Car Mark III there was the 'Car, Light Reconnaissance, Canadian GM Mark I' nicknamed the 'Otter'. A restored example is shown here in a European military museum. (*Pierre-Olivier Buan*)

Being serviced in a French barn is a Morris Armoured Reconnaissance Car AC9 of the British Expeditionary Force (BEF). This is taking place prior to the German military invasion of France in the summer of 1940. The vehicle had a length of 15ft 7in and a width of 6ft. Its height was 7ft 4in with a maximum armour thickness of 9.6mm. (*Tank Museum*)

Pictured at a museum is this example of the 4 × 4 Morris Mark II employed by the British army and the Armoured Car Companies of the RAF. It is missing any display armament. The vehicle is 13ft 3.5in in length and has a width of 6ft 8in. Its height is 6ft 2in with a maximum armour thickness of 14mm. (*Pierre-Olivier Buan*)

One of the most well-known British wheeled armoured vehicles was the Daimler Scout Car. It is best known by the unofficial nickname of 'Dingo'. The restored example pictured is being operated during a museum event. It has a length of 10ft 5in, a width of 5ft 8in and a height of 4ft 11in. Maximum armour protection on the front of the vehicle was a respectable 30mm. Its off-road mobility was excellent due to an independent suspension system. (*Ian Wilcox*)

(*Above*) On display at an Israeli army museum is a Canadian-built 4 × 4 Car Scout Ford II also known as the 'Lynx'. It was based on the design of the Daimler Scout Car known as the Dingo. The Lynx is 12ft 1.5in in length, has a width of 6ft 1in and a height of 5ft 10in. It has a maximum armour thickness of 30mm and a top speed of 50mph. (*Vladimir Yakubov*)

(*Opposite above*) Taking part in a historical military vehicle event is this restored 4 × 4 Humber Scout Car Mark II. It is 12ft 7in long and 6ft 2.5in wide. The vehicle height is 6ft 11.5in with a maximum armour protection of only 14mm. Off-road mobility of the Humber Scout Car was poor due to its commercial truck-type suspension system. (*Christophe Vallier*)

(*Opposite below*) The restored Daimler Armoured Car Mark II pictured is 13ft long and 8ft wide with a height of 7ft 4in. The maximum armour thickness on both the Mark I and Mark II versions of the vehicle is only 16mm. Like the Daimler Scout Car series upon which it was based, it had an independent suspension that provided it with excellent off-road mobility. (*Christophe Vallier*)

(*Opposite above*) The 4 × 4 Humber Armoured Car Mark III seen here in this wartime image was actually built by the British firm of Karrier Ltd rather than the firm of Humber. Both firms were subsidiaries of the British Rootes Group. It was decided to attach the name 'Humber' to the armoured car rather than 'Karrier' as it might be confused with other vehicles in British and Commonwealth army service labelled as carriers. (*Tank Museum*)

(*Opposite below*) On display is this 4 × 4 Humber Armoured Car Mark III. Unlike the Daimler Armoured Car series, the Humber Armoured Car series rode on a conventional truck-type suspension system that limited its off-road capabilities. The vehicle has a length of 15ft and a width of 7ft 2in. Its height is 7ft 10in with a maximum armour thickness of 15mm. (*Christophe Vallier*)

(*Above*) Pictured is a privately-owned 4 × 4 Canadian-built Fox Armoured Car Mark I. It is a general copy of the Humber Armoured Car Mark III. Instead of employing a British chassis and powertrain for the Fox, the Canadians went with an American chassis and powertrain upon which they mounted an armoured hull and turret very similar to its British counterpart. (*Christophe Vallier*)

(*Opposite above*) The British army 4 × 4 Coventry Armoured Car pictured was armed with a turret-mounted 2-pounder cannon and a machine gun. It had a length of 15ft 6in and a width of 8ft 9in. The vehicle height was 7ft 9in with a maximum armour thickness of 14mm. As with the Daimler Armoured car series, the Coventry rode on an advance independent suspension system. (*Tank Museum*)

(*Above*) On display is a 4 × 4 ACE Armoured Car Mark II armed with a 6-pounder cannon and machine gun. Like so many other British-designed and built armoured cars that were constructed in great haste during the early war years it was based on a commercial 4 × 4 truck chassis. Despite this and lacking an independent suspension system, the ACE was well-thought-of by the British army. (*Tank Museum*)

(*Opposite below*) A wartime image of a British army 4 × 4 ACE Armoured Car Mark II being cheered by the local inhabitants, no doubt pleased to be free of a German military presence. Powered by a diesel engine rather than the gasoline version of most other British armoured cars, the vehicle had a length of 17ft and a width of 9ft. Its height was 8ft 4in and maximum armour thickness on the vehicle was 57mm. (*Tank Museum*)

(*Opposite above*) The standard armament on the South African-built 4 × 4 Mark II Armoured Reconnaissance Car consisted of a machine gun and an anti-tank rifle. Those units issued with the vehicle found it under-gunned when compared to its Axis counterparts. This led to some of them having their turrets removed as pictured here and armed with captured enemy weapons, in this case an Italian 20mm automatic cannon. (*Tank Museum*)

(*Opposite below*) Pictured on patrol in this wartime image is a South African-built 4 × 4 Mark III Armoured Reconnaissance Car. It was 16ft in length with a width of 6ft 6in and the vehicle height was 7ft 3in. Maximum armour thickness topped out at 12mm. Besides its use by the South African army, it and others in the series were also employed by the British army. (*Tank Museum*)

(*Above*) To overcome the firepower disadvantage of the South African-built 4 × 4 Mark III Armoured Reconnaissance Car, a redesigned and up-gunned vehicle they labelled as the Mark IV came into service in 1942. Its main armament was a 2-pounder cannon. Eventually a machine gun was added. A preserved example of a South African-built Mark IV Armoured Reconnaissance Car is pictured here. (*Ian Wilcox*)

(*Above*) South African industry never ceased its wartime efforts in building armoured cars that could match the capabilities of their German counterparts. This led to a number of developmental projects of which only the Mark VI version was considered for production. However, in the end only two prototypes were constructed, one of which had as its main armament a 6-pounder cannon and is seen here. (*Tank Museum*)

(*Opposite above*) In this wartime image we see an open-topped 4 × 4 India Pattern Carrier in use by the British army. The vehicle had a length of 15ft 6in, a width of 7ft 5in and a height of 6ft 6in. Its maximum armour thickness was 14mm. As it rode on a commercial truck-type suspension system, its off-road capabilities were limited. (*Tank Museum*)

(*Opposite below*) Australian industry designed and built for the US Army Air Forces (AAF) units based in the country during the Second World War a fairly crude open-topped 4 × 4 armoured vehicle intended for airfield defence. It was assigned the US army designation S-1 Scout Car as seen in this official photograph. It is reported that approximately forty of these were built. (*TACOM*)

Belonging to a private collector is this restored British-built Universal Carrier. The vehicle is 12ft long, has a width of 7ft and a height of 5ft 3in. It has a maximum speed of 30mph and an approximate operational range of 140 miles. Maximum armour thickness is only 10mm. It could overcome a 2ft vertical obstacle and cross a gap measuring 4ft 6in. *(Author's collection)*

A Universal Carrier is seen here in the service of a Red Army reconnaissance unit. It is armed with an anti-tank rifle seen protruding from the front of the vehicle's hull and a small-calibre British-built machine gun named the 'Bren'. In total, the Red Army received 2,008 units of the Universal Carrier, which included both British and Canadian-built examples. *(Bob Fleming)*

Taking part in a demonstration is a turretless American-built M5 Light Tank in British army markings. It is replicating the British army policy that began during the Italian campaign of using turretless American light tanks as reconnaissance vehicles. These turretless machine-gun-armed tanks were nicknamed the 'Stuart Recce' as the British army had already named the M3 and M5 series of light tanks acquired under Lend-Lease as the 'Stuart'. *(Christophe Vallier)*

The restored 4 × 4 Staghound armoured car pictured here is 18ft in length, has a width of 8ft 10in and a height of 7ft 9in. Maximum armour protection on the vehicle is 32mm. It is powered by two gasoline engines that give it a top speed on level roads of 56mph. It had authorized storage for 103 rounds for its 37mm M6 main gun.

(Michel Krauss)

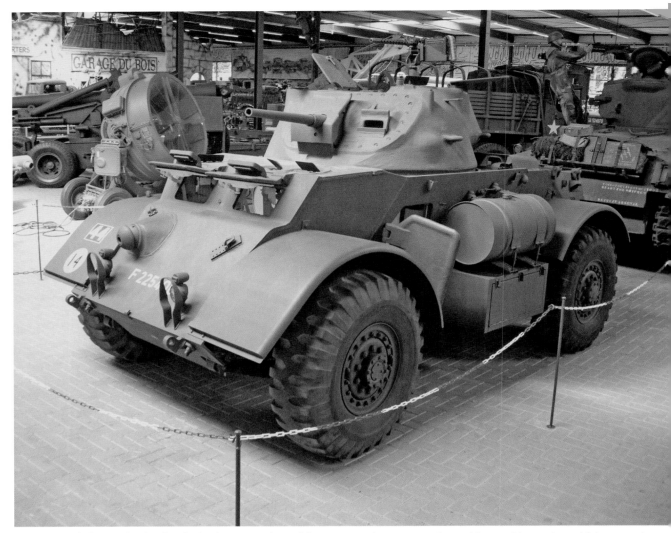

(*Above*) On display is a Staghound armoured car. After overcoming some early teething problems, the vehicle proved extremely reliable in service. The New Zealand army units issued with the armoured car during the Italian campaign felt that the vehicle was under-gunned. In an effort to redress that issue some were armed with a British-built 3-inch howitzer in place of its normal 37mm M6 Gun and referred to as the 'Staghound II'. (*Pierre-Olivier Buan*)

(*Opposite above*) The British army was interested at one point in time in another American-designed and built medium armoured car they named the 'Deerhound'. The US army designation for the vehicle was the T17 as seen in this official photograph. It was a 6 × 6 vehicle that had a length of 18ft 2in, a width of 8ft 6in and a height of 9ft. (*TACOM*)

(*Opposite below*) On display is the armoured car the British army named the 'Boarhound' and the US army designated as the Heavy Armoured Car T18E2. Despite early interest in the 8 × 8 vehicle by both the US army and the British army, neither would take it into service. The massive vehicle is 20ft 6in in length, 10ft 1in in width and has a height of 8ft 7in. (*Tank Museum*)

(*Opposite above*) A somewhat worse-for-wear French-built 4 × 2 AMD Laffly 50 AM armoured car is pictured here. It had a length of 17ft 7in, a width of 7ft 6.5in and a height of 8ft 1.5in. Maximum armour thickness on the vehicle was 7mm. It had a top speed on roads of 43mph and could cross a trench 16in wide. (*Tank Museum*)

(*Above*) The armoured half-track pictured is a French army AMC Schneider P16. The large roller on the front of the vehicle was intended to assist it in crossing uneven terrain. The vehicle commander/gunner was located in the turret. The length of the AMC Schneider P16 was 15ft 10in, it had a width of 5ft 8in and the vehicle height was 8ft 6in. Maximum armour thickness was 11.4mm. (*Tank Museum*)

(*Opposite below*) The French army's replacement for the AMC Schneider P16 was the AMD 35 seen here in a French museum. It had a driver in both the front and rear of the vehicle's hull. The vehicle had a maximum armour thickness of 20mm. It was 15ft 8.5in long and 6ft 6in wide with a height of 7ft 6in. (*Author's collection*)

(*Above*) The Red Army began to field the machine-gun-armed 4 × 2 BA-20 Light Armoured Car seen here in a pre-Second World War parade in 1936. The BA-20 in the foreground is radio-equipped as is evident from its metal frame antenna around the uppermost portion of its hull. The chassis of the BA-20 was derived from a 1933 Ford Motors-designed and built car that they referred to as the GAZ-M1. (*Tank Museum*)

(*Opposite page*) Following the three Red Army motorcyclists there are at least two 4 × 2 BA-20 Light Armoured Cars in this wartime photograph. Maximum armour thickness on the light armoured car was 10mm. It was 14ft 2in in length, had a width of 5ft 9in and the vehicle height was 7ft. Maximum speed on level roads was 53mph. (*Bob Fleming*)

(*Right*) On display at a Moscow military museum is this preserved 6 × 4 BA-6 Heavy Armoured Car. It is armed with a 45mm gun-armed turret. Not seen in this picture is the front hull-mounted small-calibre machine gun. The aperture where it would have been fitted has been covered by a circular metal plate on this museum vehicle. (*Vladimir Yakubov*)

(*Opposite above*) A wartime image of two destroyed Red Army 6 × 4 BA-10A Heavy Armoured Cars. A key external difference between the BA-6 and the BA-10A is the smaller conical turret on the latter. Like the BA-6 the BA-10 was armed with a 45mm gun and two machine guns, with one in the front hull. The maximum armour thickness on the vehicle was bumped up to 15mm. (*Author's collection*)

(*Above*) On display is this somewhat worse-for-wear 4 × 4 BA-64B Light Armoured Car that had formerly been on display at the now-closed US Army Ordnance Museum. The Soviet designers were obviously influenced by examining captured examples of German 4 × 4 light armoured cars. The chassis of the BA-64 series was constructed on the GAZ-64 Light Cross Country Car. (*Paul Hannah*)

(*Opposite below*) Crew members stand at attention during a parade formation of Red Army BA-64B Light Armoured Cars. The vehicle had a length of 12ft, a width of 5ft and a height of 6ft 3in. The gasoline engine of the A-64 series gave it a maximum speed on level roads of 50mph and an operational range of approximately 375 miles. The maximum armour thickness of the vehicle was 10mm. (*Bob Fleming*)

Prior to being accepted for service in 1934 the US army's 6 × 4 M1 Armoured Car was labelled as the T4 Armoured Car. That fact is announced on the sign attached to the vehicle's hull in this photograph. Maximum armour thickness was 13mm. The M1 Armoured Car had a length of 15ft and a width of 6ft with a height of 6ft 11in. (*Patton Museum*)

In 1935 the US army acquired the first of its M1 Scout Cars as seen here. The markings on the vehicle shown and the radio antenna indicate that it is being employed as a command vehicle. It was powered by a gasoline engine, as were all subsequent US army scout cars. Note the running board, a feature commonly seen on commercial vehicles of the time. (*Patton Museum*)

In 1938 the US army took into service the 4 × 4 M2 Scout Car seen here. As with the earlier M1 Scout Car, the M2 Scout Car was designed with as many commercial truck components as possible to keep costs down. Maximum armour thickness was 12.7mm. It had a length of 15ft 11in, a width of 6ft 8.5in and a height of 6ft 1.5in. *(Patton Museum)*

Following on the heels of the 4 × 4 M2 Scout Car appeared the improved Scout Car M2A1, which was quickly redesignated as the M3 Scout Car by the US army. The maximum armour thickness on the vehicle was 25mm on the armoured cover that was lowered over the front windshield. The remainder of the vehicle was protected by armour plate some 13mm thick. *(Patton Museum)*

With some tweaking of the design, the M3 Scout Car was replaced by the very similar M3A1 Scout Car. A restored example of an M3A1 is seen here in early-war US army markings. As is evident from the picture, a major identifying feature of the M3A1 was the widening of the hull compared to the earlier M3 Scout Car. The vehicle had a top speed on level roads of 50mph. (*Chris Hughes*)

Unlike the M3 Scout Car the M3A1 version lacked a rear door as is evident from this picture. As with the M2 the machine-gun armament of the M3A1 was attached to mounts that could be moved around the interior of the vehicle by way of a skate rail visible in this image. Typically mounted on the rear of the M3A1 but not seen here would be the ground tripods for its machine guns. (*Patton Museum*)

Employed in the reconnaissance role by the US army prior to Pearl Harbor and during America's early involvement in the Second World War was the M2 Half-Track Armoured Car. As it was intended as a multi-purpose vehicle, it had two large storage bins on either side of the vehicle just behind the driver's compartment. The open hatch for the one on the left side of the vehicle is visible in this picture. *(TACOM)*

Another armoured half-track pressed into the reconnaissance role by the US army during the initial stages of the Second World War was the M3 Half-Track Personnel Carrier. The example pictured is taking part in a training exercise. The M3 Half-Track Personnel Carrier was longer than the M2 Half-Track Armoured Car and could therefore carry more passengers. *(Patton Museum)*

(*Opposite above*) Pictured is the Ford Motors 6 × 6 pilot vehicle labelled as the T22 Light Armoured Car. It was delivered to the US army before a competitor's submissions were ready for testing. In a rush to introduce into service an armoured car that could be built cheaply and in large numbers, the US army skipped testing of the competitor's vehicles and went ahead and ordered a modified version of the Ford T22 into production as the 6 × 6 M8 Light Armoured Car. (*TACOM*)

(*Opposite below*) An official wartime photograph of a fully-stowed 6 × 6 M8 Light Armoured Car with its turret-mounted large-calibre machine gun covered by a foul-weather canvas cover. The M8 lacked the front hull-mounted small-calibre machine gun present on the T22 Light Armoured Car pilot vehicle. However, it was fitted with self-sealing fuel tanks, a feature not found on the T22. (*TACOM*)

(*Above*) Pictured during a historical military vehicle event is a restored M8 Light Armoured Car. Unlike the pilot T22 Light Armoured Car that had a cast armour turret, the M8 had a welded armour turret. The M8 was powered by the same gasoline engine as the M3A1 Scout Car and had an even poorer degree of off-road mobility. A particular weak spot was the front leaf springs of the vehicle. (*Author's collection*)

(*Opposite above*) A restored M8 Light Armoured Car in Free French army markings. One of the many concerns for the wartime crews of the M8 was the lack of an armoured floor, leaving them vulnerable to mines. This issue was typically resolved by lining the vehicle's floor with multiple layers of sandbags. However, the extra weight of the sandbags unfortunately caused problems with the vehicle's suspension system. (*Christophe Vallier*)

(*Opposite below*) In this wartime photograph we see a US army M8 Light Armoured Car. Due to its thin armour and limited firepower, the M8 was intended to acquire information by stealth and only fight when no other option was available. However, the armoured car's 37mm M6 Gun firing canister and the large-calibre machine gun with which it was typically fitted could be extremely effective against unprotected enemy infantry. (*Patton Museum*)

(*Above*) On display at a historical military vehicle event is a restored 6 × 6 M8 Light Armoured Car. The vehicle is 16ft 5in in length, has a width of 8ft 4in and a height of 7ft 4in. The vehicle's gasoline engine gave it a top road speed of 55mph and an approximate operational range of 350 miles. Maximum armour protection on the vehicle was 19mm. (*Christophe Vallier*)

(*Opposite above*) From the beginning it was envisioned by the US army that there would be a number of derivatives of the 6 × 6 M8 Light Armoured Car placed into service. In the end only the turretless 6 × 6 M20 Armoured Utility Vehicle was ordered into production. The restored M20 pictured here is taking part in a historical military vehicle event held at the now-closed Patton Museum of Armor and Cavalry. (*Chun-lun Hsu*)

(*Opposite below*) The planned US army replacement for the 6 × 6 M8 Light Armoured Car was the 6 × 6 T27/M38 Light Armoured Car pictured here. Unlike the simple truck-type suspension system of the former, the latter had been fitted with a more advanced independently-sprung suspension system. With the British army anticipating that they would receive the M38 under Lend-Lease, they assigned it the name 'Wolfhound'. (*TACOM*)

(*Above*) A number of developmental projects were undertaken during the war years to come up with an armoured Jeep for the reconnaissance role but all failed because the Jeep chassis could not support the weight. However, this did not stop the troops in the field from building their own improvised-armour Jeeps as seen in this wartime picture. (*Patton Museum*)

Chapter Two

Tank Destroyers

Most of the Allied armies of the Second World War believed that the best tank-killing weapon was another tank. The exception to that was the US army, which decided in May 1941 that tanks were to be reserved for the exploitation role. If enemy tanks were to be encountered in large numbers by US army armoured divisions, yet-to-be-fielded vehicle-mounted anti-tank guns named 'tank destroyers' were to be rushed forward to deal with the threat.

The US army's decision to embrace the concept of specialized tank destroyers was based on the unfounded belief that the highly-thought-of pre-war French army had been overwhelmed and defeated by masses of German tanks in the summer of 1940. In reality, the German army did not have a clear superiority in tank numbers over their opponents during that campaign. In addition, the German army armoured divisions fought in combined arms team and not in all-tank formations.

The First Tank Destroyer

As it was felt that time was of the essence and there was nothing in the inventory to equip the planned new tank destroyer units, it was decided by the US army as an experiment in June 1941 to mount a modernized First World War-vintage field gun designated as the 75mm Gun M1897A4 on the chassis of an M3 Half-Track Personnel Carrier. The resulting pilot vehicle was designated as the 75mm GMC (Gun Motor Carriage) T12.

The T12 worked well enough as an interim tank destroyer for eighty-six units to be delivered to the US army between August and September 1941. In October 1941, a revised version of the vehicle was designated as the 75mm GMC M3. It was followed into production by another version with a different gun mount designated as the 75mm GMC M3A1. A total of 2,116 units of the approximately 20,000lb 75mm GMC M3/M3A1 series were delivered to the US army between February 1942 and April 1943.

Combat Use

Some of the T12s and 75mm GMC M3 vehicles were shipped to the Philippines prior to the Japanese attack on Pearl Harbor. They would see combat against the invading

Japanese army between December 1941 and May 1942. A number of tank destroyer units equipped with the 75mm GMC M3 also saw combat with the US army during the fighting in North Africa that took place between November 1942 and May 1943. Results were not positive and would lead to serious doubts about the entire concept of tank destroyers.

The 75mm GMC M3s that took part in the US army's Italian campaign (July 1943 till May 1945) served as self-propelled artillery pieces. The British army would also adopt a limited number of the vehicles during the Italian campaign to offer fire support to some of its armoured car units. As the remaining 75mm GMC M3 series vehicles became redundant to US army requirements many were converted back to their original role as personnel carriers.

Lend-Lease Half-Track Tank Destroyer

Another American-built half-track-based tank destroyer was the 19,000lb 57mm GMC T48. Like the T12 and the 75mm GMC M3 series, it was based on the M3 Half-Track Personnel Carrier. It was armed with the 57mm Gun M1, which was a modified version of the British-designed 6-pounder cannon. A total of 962 units of the vehicle were built between December 1942 and May 1943.

The American-built T48 had originally been designed and built to satisfy a British army requirement as none existed in the US army. However, upon their completion the British army no longer had a requirement for the T48. They therefore passed on 650 units of the vehicle to the Red Army, kept 30 for themselves and let the US army retain the remaining 282 units. The British army converted their thirty units of the T48 back to the half-track personnel carrier configuration, as did the US army with all but one example.

Tank Destroyer Dead-Ends

In January 1942, the US army gave approval for the production of 1,580 units of a vehicle labelled as the 3-inch GMC M5. It consisted of an armoured, shield-protected 3-inch gun designated as the M5 mounted on the modified but unarmoured chassis of a full-tracked aircraft-towing vehicle designated as the High-Speed Tractor M2 by the US army.

Despite only minimal testing that had raised some early misgivings regarding the 3-inch GMC M5's durability as a tank destroyer, the vehicle's production had the support of a very senior US army general that overcame any objections for a time. Fortunately for the US army, subsequent testing of the 3-inch GMC M5 revealed some serious design flaws that led to the vehicle being cancelled in August 1942 before production commenced.

The US army had also explored the concept of mounting the 3-inch Gun M5 on an open-topped armoured chassis of the Light Tank M3. This experimental combination was labelled as the 3-inch GMC T20. However, it and other projects using modified light tanks such as the M3A3 to mount a 3-inch Gun M5 were eventually cancelled because none could support the weight and recoil of the weapon.

Another tank destroyer dead-end that actually made it into production was the 37mm GMC M6. It consisted of a 37mm Gun M6 mounted in the rear cargo bay of a 4 × 4 Dodge WC-55 Truck already in service with the US army. The only armour protection on the vehicle was the weapon's gun shield. A total of 5,380 units of the approximately 7,000lb M6 were built between April and October 1942.

Although originally thought of only as a training vehicle, some of the four-man M6s were shipped with the US army to North Africa. Those units issued with the vehicle had no illusions about its combat usefulness. Most were quickly de-gunned and saw more productive use as transport vehicles. Some of the 37mm guns stripped off the M6 units in North Africa were re-mounted on the multi-purpose M2 Half-track Cars or M3 Half-track Personnel Carriers.

Tank-Based Tank Destroyers

In September 1941, the US army began exploring the possibility of mounting the 3-inch Anti-Aircraft Gun M3 in a fixed forward-firing position on the open-topped chassis of the Medium Tank M3. The following month the proposed tank destroyer was labelled as the 3-inch GMC T24. Testing of a pilot example began in November 1941.

The Japanese attack on Pearl Harbor in December 1941 prompted the US army to authorize the production of thirty units of the T24, which was therefore assigned the designation 3-inch GMC M9. The Tank Destroyer Command formed in November 1941 rejected the vehicle as their interest was being diverted to the idea of placing the new 3-inch Gun M7 in a new open-topped turret design mounted on the chassis of the Medium Tank M4A2.

Combat reports from US army units fighting the Japanese army in the Philippines in December 1941 and January 1942 indicated that sloped armour could be helpful in deflecting a wider range of projectiles. This led to the construction of two pilot vehicles in April 1942, both based on the chassis of the Medium Tank M4A2. One had horizontal side and rear hull armour and was labelled as the 3-inch GMC T35. The other was modified with sloped side and rear hull armour and was designated as the 3-inch GMC T35E1.

The M10 Tank Destroyer Appears

In June 1942, the US army ordered the 3-inch GMC T35E1 into production as the 3-inch GMC M10. Rather than the original open-topped cast armour turret that came with the T35E1, the M10 rolled off the assembly line with an open-topped welded armour turret. This was done because the welded armour turret offered a superior degree of ballistic protection. The open-topped turret design of the M10 was used to improve the crew's visibility in combat.

To keep the weight of the M10 down, the armour on the vehicle's hull was thinner than that of the Medium Tank M4A2. Mobility was still assigned a much higher design priority than firepower by the senior general overseeing the Tank Destroyer Force. This was done despite the US army Ordnance Department warning that more heavily-armoured German tanks would no doubt be encountered in the future and might be immune to the projectiles fired by the 3-inch Gun M7 on the M10.

A total of 4,993 units of the M10 were constructed between September 1942 and December 1943. As a consequence of concerns that there would not be enough of the M4A2 chassis units available to convert into the M10, authorization was given to use the chassis of the Medium Tank M4A3 for building another version of the vehicle referred to as the 3-inch GMC M10A1. In total 1,713 units of the M10A1 were built.

The M10 in Combat

Two battalions of M10s were deployed to North Africa and saw action between March and May 1943. However, their only employment in the tank destroyer role occurred during the first month of their arrival in theatre. For the remainder of their time in theatre they were used as self-propelled artillery pieces. This was due to the reluctance of local field commanders to hold them in the rear awaiting the mass German tank attacks that never took place.

The M10s would also be employed as self-propelled artillery pieces during the Italian campaign due to the small number of German tanks encountered. By the time M10s were being deployed to the European Theatre of Operation (ETO) in the summer of 1944, they had also been assigned the assault gun (infantry support) role. This was in addition to their occasional role as self-propelled artillery pieces.

It was in the ETO during June and July of 1944 that the US army became painfully aware of the fact that the 3-inch Gun M7 on the M10 lacked the penetrative power to destroy late-war German tanks like the Panther. This pushed all concerned to demand a better-armed tank destroyer to replace the M10. New superior armour-piercing rounds for the 3-inch main gun on the M10 appeared in late 1944. However, these improved rounds were always in short supply.

The M10 was also assigned to the Pacific Theatre of Operation (PTO) where the lack of Japanese tanks meant that its primary role was as an assault gun. As in the ETO, the open-topped turret of the M10 and its thin armour made it unpopular with its crews in the assault gun role as it left them extremely vulnerable to enemy mortar and artillery fire. Another threat to the M10 in the PTO was close-in attacks by Japanese infantry carrying hand-held explosive devices.

Another Tank Destroyer Failure

Following the M10 into US army service was the five-man 76mm GMC M18. It had been authorized for production in March 1944 and was armed with either the 76mm Gun M1A1 or M1A2. These were the same main guns mounted on the second generation of M4 series medium tanks. In the ETO it soon became clear that these guns could not be counted on to destroy German late-war tanks from the front at normal combat ranges.

At one point it was envisioned that the US army would require 7,386 units of the approximately 40,000lb M18 and that another 1,600 units would be reserved for the British and Soviets under Lend-Lease. By the time production of the M18 commenced, the entire concept of tank destroyers had already been discredited. This in turn led to orders for the M18 being dramatically reduced. Only 2,507 units were built, with none being accepted by the British or the Red Army.

The Best-Armed Tank Destroyer

The US army's answer to the combat failure of the M10 and M18 turned out to be the five-man 90mm GMC M36 that first showed up in the ETO in October 1944. It consisted of the modified chassis of the M10A1 fitted with a newly-designed open-topped turret. The 90mm Gun M3 on the approximately 62,000lb M36 was the same as that fitted on the approximately 92,000lb Heavy Tank M26 that did not arrive in the ETO until January 1945.

The main gun on the M36 was a major improvement over the main guns of the M10 and M18 but still could not reliably penetrate the front hull armour plate (glacis) on the German Panther tank at over 500 yards. The introduction of new AP ammunition in late 1944 did improve the weapon's penetrative performance but this was always in scarce supply.

The US army's encounter with the German Tiger B Heavy Tank during the Battle of the Bulge led to the demand for even more M36s to replace the remaining M10s in the ETO. Because the supply of M10A1s was being exhausted, it was decided to convert M10s into the M36 configuration. This version of the vehicle was designated as the M36B2 and 827 units were completed.

American Tank Destroyers in Foreign Service

Of the 4,993 units of the M10 built by American industry, a total of 1,648 units were supplied to the British army under Lend-Lease. In their service they were labelled as the 3-inch Self-Propelled Mount (SPM) M10 Mark I or II. The distinction between marks was the type of rear turret counterweight with which they were equipped.

Not impressed with the penetrative power of the 3-inch Gun M7 on the M10s supplied to them, the British army decided to re-arm the 3-inch SPM Mark II with the more powerful British-designed and built Ordnance, QF, 17-pounder gun. The up-arming process began in May 1944 and continued until April 1945, with 1,017 units completed.

The re-armed M10s were designated as the M10C or the M10 17-Pounder by the British army. Despite the widespread belief that the M10C was officially nicknamed the 'Achilles', this was not the case and does not show up in any British army documents from the Second World War.

Besides the British army, the original American-supplied version of the M10 and the up-gunned model would serve with various Commonwealth armies. Some went to the Polish forces fighting for the Western Allies. The Red Army received fifty-two M10s under Lend-Lease. The Free French army was supplied 155 units of the M10 under Lend-Lease. They acquired another 100 or more M10s from US army stock-piles in North-West Europe.

The only successful mounting of the 17-pounder on a British tank chassis was officially nicknamed the 'Archer'. It consisted of the gun being mounted on the reworked and turretless chassis of redundant Valentine light tanks. The weapon itself was installed on a mount with limited traverse in an open-topped armoured compartment at the front of the vehicle. A total of 665 units of the Archer were built between March 1944 and the end of the war in Europe.

Gun Truck Tank Destroyers

The French army decided in late 1939 to begin the construction of a 6 × 6 armoured gun truck fitted with an armoured cab and a shield-protected 47mm SA35 anti-tank gun on its rear deck. It was labelled as the Laffly TCC and the seventy units built prior to the German invasion in the summer of 1940 proved effective in battle.

Sometime during the fighting in North Africa in 1943, the Free French army mounted a shield-protected 75mm M1897 on the rear deck of a 4 × 4 Ford truck and labelled it as the 'BB3 Conus Gun'. The number built is unknown. The British and Commonwealth armies fighting in North Africa also took to mounting on the rear decks of standard 4 × 4 American or British-built cargo trucks shield-protected 2-pounder or 6-pounder towed anti-tank guns.

The British army also developed a better-protected gun truck to perform the role of tank destroyer. That vehicle was named the 'Deacon', with its official designation being AEC Mark I Gun Carrier. It was a 6 × 6 armoured truck that was armed with a 6-pounder gun on its rear cargo deck protected by an armoured enclosure. A total of 175 units of the Deacon were built in 1942 and would see action in North Africa up until May 1943 when it was replaced by more advanced tank destroyers.

Australian Tank Destroyer

Australian industry, in response to the needs of their own country's army, set about the design and development of a suitable tank destroyer in 1942. Rather than using a wheeled chassis, the decision was made to mount a 2-pounder gun on the lengthened chassis of a licence-built copy of the British-designed Universal Carrier.

The modified Australian copy of the Universal Carrier was designated the LP2 Carrier. With the weapon fitted the vehicle was designated as the 2-pounder Anti-Tank Gun Carrier. A total of 200 units of the approximately 11,000lb vehicle were built with none seeing combat. Their only wartime employment was as training vehicles in Australia as by the time they reached production the 2-pounder gun was considered obsolete.

Red Army Tank Destroyers

During the Second World War the Red Army fielded two dedicated tank destroyers. These were the SU-85 and the follow-on SU-100. Both were turretless vehicles with their main guns fitted to fire forward from an armoured casemate located on the frontal portion of the vehicle with limited traverse and elevation. Both were based on the chassis of the T-34 series medium tank. The 85mm main gun on the SU-85 was designated as the D-5S and the 100mm main gun on the SU-100 as the D-10S.

The SU-85 entered into production in July 1943. It was the Red Army antidote to the German army's fielding of relatively large numbers of Tiger E Heavy Tanks and Panther tanks in the summer of 1943. In the role of tank destroyer the approximately 65,000lb SU-85 assumed the over-watch position to protect the less well-armed first-generation T-34 series tanks armed with a 76.2mm main gun. Lacking any machine-gun armament, the vehicle was not suitable for close-in fighting.

Production of the four-man SU-85 was discontinued in the summer of 1944 with 2,652 units built. Of that number, 315 units had been built upon the follow-on tank destroyer and labeled as the SU-85M. This occurred because the second-generation T-34 series tank armed with an 85mm main gun and labelled as the T34-85 began to enter front-line service in large numbers. The four-man SU-100 took over the role of the SU-85. Production of the approximately 70,000lb vehicle began in September 1944 and continued into early 1946 with 3,037 units constructed.

(*Opposite above*) The initial configuration of the 75mm GMC T12 had the three-man gun crew protected only by the small flat armoured gun shield as seen here. The 75mm gun fitted to the T12 was the 75mm gun M1897A4. It was provided with an armour-piercing round that in theory could penetrate 3.2in of armour sloped at 20 degrees. (*Patton Museum*)

(*Opposite below*) To provide additional protection for the 75mm GMC T12 gun crew, a number of different gun shield configurations were experimented with including the high-profile example seen in this photograph. The 75mm gun M1897A4 fitted to the T12 had a rate of fire of six rounds per minute with a well-trained crew. In addition to its armour-piercing round it could also fire a high-explosive round. (*Patton Museum*)

(*Opposite above*) The US army eventually decided on the low-profile gun shield seen in this picture for both the 75mm GMC T12 and the follow-on 75mm GMC M3 pictured here. The vehicles had room for fifty-nine main gun rounds. The maximum protection on the front of the vehicles was the armoured window shield at 12.7mm. This shield folded down when the gun was to be fired. (*National Archives*)

(*Opposite below*) The vehicle crew of the T12 had been four men but it was decided that this was not sufficient and the crew of the 75mm GMC M3 consisted of five men as pictured. These included the driver, assistant driver (radio-operator), gun commander, gunner and loader. Note that the loader had to hunch down prior to the weapon being fired to make room for the breech to recoil. (*Patton Museum*)

(*Above*) Pictured is a replica 75mm GMC M3 in Second World War Marine Corps markings. The vehicle and gun are original but the gun mount and gun shield are reproductions. Rather than serving as a tank destroyer, the 75mm GMC M3 in US Marine Corps service was typically employed as an infantry support assault gun or as a self-propelled artillery piece. (*National Archives*)

As the supply of 75mm gun M1897A4s was being exhausted and there was still some thought about continuing the production of the 75mm GMC M3, it was decided to see if the 75mm main gun mounted in the first generation of M4 series medium tanks could be modified to be fitted Into the 75mm GMC M3A1. The pilot vehicle built to prove that the concept was workable is shown here in September 1943. It was designated as the 75mm GMC T73. However, by the time it was ready for testing there were more suitable tank destroyers in production and the project was cancelled by the US army. (TACOM)

The successful creation of the 75mm GMC M3 led the US army to offer the British army a similar vehicle pictured here designated the 57mm GMC T48. As events transpired, the bulk of those built were shipped under Lend-Lease to the Soviet Union and not to Great Britain. In Red Army service the vehicle was designated as the SU-57 and organized into special independent tank destroyer units. (Bob Fleming)

Pictured is the 3-inch GMC M5. The weapon mounted on the chassis was the 3-inch gun M6. Like all those 3-inch guns before and after it, the design can be traced back to the 3-inch Gun M1903 originally employed as a coastal defence weapon. It was redesigned to become an anti-aircraft gun during the First World War and eventually became an anti-tank gun during the Second World War. (*Patton Museum*)

In an attempt to find a full-tracked chassis that could support the weight and recoil of a 3-inch gun, the weapon was at one point mounted as an experiment on a much-modified M3A3 Light Tank. In the test configuration pictured here the vehicle was assigned the designation 3-inch GMC T56. To provide a fighting compartment for the gun crew at the rear of the vehicle the engine was moved to the middle of the hull. (*TACOM*)

In this dramatically-staged photograph the crew of this 37mm GMC M6 is demonstrating potential fighting positions on the vehicle. The vehicle's onboard weapon was designated as the 37mm Anti-tank Gun M3 and could only be fired over the rear cargo bay of the vehicle. It had a muzzle velocity of 2,900 feet per second when firing an armour-piercing round. (*Patton Museum*)

The shield-protected 37mm anti-tank guns from de-gunned 37mm GMC M6s were remounted in some cases on armoured half-tracks. Pictured here is an example of this practice in England prior to the Normandy invasion in June 1944. The M2 Half-Track Car belongs to the 41st Armoured Infantry Regiment that formed part of the 2nd Armoured Division.

(*Patton Museum*)

Weight empty: 51,605 lbs.
Weight loaded: 54,600 lbs.
Turning Diameter 68 ft.
Max. Height 8 ft. 7 in.
Height of bore above ground
zero elevation 7 ft. 8 in.

Maximum elevation of gun 15°
Maximum depression 2°
Maximum traverse right 16½°, left 16½°
Rounds of ammunition 40
Crew 6

The US army's biggest problem early on was in finding a full-tracked chassis that could support the weight and recoil of a 3-inch gun. As an interim measure it was proposed in September 1941 that the 3-inch Gun M3 be mounted on the open-topped armoured chassis of the M3 Medium Tank. That vehicle seen here during testing in November 1941 was designated as the 3-inch GMC T24 but was rejected as it was too tall and lacked the required traverse. A follow-on vehicle designated as the 3-inch GMC T24 or M9 was also cancelled for the same reasons. (TACOM)

The US army wanted a tank destroyer armed with a 3-inch gun mounted in a turret capable of 360 degrees traverse. Two pilots based on a modified M4A2 Medium Tank chassis with a new open-topped turret design were evaluated. The example seen here with vertical armour hull plates was designated as the 3-inch GMC T35. The other pilot had a sloped hull armour arrangement and was labelled as the 3-inch GMC T35E1. (TACOM)

It was decided by the US army to take advantage of the superior ballistic protection offered by the sloped armour hull arrangement of the 3-inch GMC T35E1. That vehicle was therefore ordered into production as the 3-inch GMC M10 with a welded armour turret as seen here on this restored example rather than the cast armour turret of the T35E1 pilot vehicle. (*Marc Sehring*)

The 3-inch GMC M10 had authorized storage for fifty-four main gun rounds. Of that number, six were stored in the open-topped turret and were referred to as 'ready rounds', three of which are seen in this illustration. The remaining forty-eight main gun rounds were stored in racks within the hull crew compartment. The M10 and M10A1 were not provided with a coaxial machine gun. (*Patton Museum*)

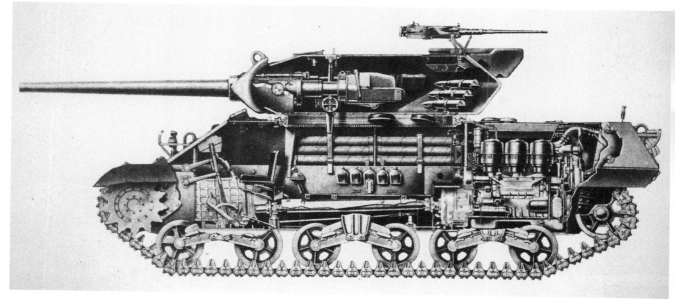

Due to the weight of the 3-inch gun the turret on the early-production units of the M10 and M10A1 proved unbalanced. To compensate for this the units in the field came up with improvised rear turret counterweights for their vehicles. The issue was finally solved by a two-piece factory-installed counterweight system seen on the rear of this M10 on display in Europe. (*Pierre-Olivier Buan*)

The US army decision to make its full-tracked tank destroyer turrets open-topped was not a popular one among those issued with the vehicles. The units in the field sometimes took it upon themselves to rectify this problem by coming up with improvised turret covers as seen here. The sides of the pentagonal-shaped turret of the M10 and M10A1 were only 25mm thick. (*Patton Museum*)

(*Above*) Pictured is an M10 on display in France. The thickest armour on the vehicle was the gun shield at 70mm. The vehicle has a length of 19.6ft, a width of 10ft and a height of 8ft 1in. It had a maximum fuel load of 192 gallons that gave it an approximate road range of 160 miles at a top speed on level roads of 30mph. (*Pierre-Olivier Buan*)

(*Opposite above*) Shown here during a historical military vehicle event is an M10 in Free French army markings. The bosses on the hull and turret of the vehicle pictured were added at the factory for all but late-production M10s. They were intended for the attachment of factory-made add-on armour kits that were never placed into production. (*Christophe Vallier*)

(*Opposite below*) The 3-inch gun mounted in the M10 seen here was officially designated as the M7. It weighed 1,990lb and had a length of 13ft. The main tank-killing round for the weapon was the M62 APC (armour-piercing, capped). The projectile portion of the round weighed approximately 15lb and in theory could penetrate 93mm of armour plate with a slope of 30 degrees at a range of 500 yards. (*Patton Museum*)

(*Above*) Pictured in the ETO is this US army M10 with the typical trappings of a vehicle in the field with the crew's sleeping bags draped over both the turret and front hull. Also visible on the front hull (glacis) are some sandbags for additional protection. On this particular vehicle the crew has moved the large-calibre machine gun from the rear of the open-topped turret to its front. (*Patton Museum*)

(*Opposite above*) The Tank Destroyer Force had been extremely unhappy with the US army forcing them to take the M10 and M10A1 into service. They had much preferred to wait for what they considered as the ultimate tank destroyer to be fielded. That vehicle started off as the 57mm GMC T49, which later evolved into the 76mm GMC T70 pictured here. (*TACOM*)

(*Opposite below*) Despite a number of design flaws with the 76mm GMC T70 that included a very short track life, the vehicle was ordered into production by the US army as the 76mm GMC M18. An example is seen here on display at the former tank museum located at the US army Ordnance School. The Ordnance School had been located at Aberdeen Proving Ground, Maryland for many decades. (*TACOM*)

(*Opposite above*) A privately-owned and restored 76mm GMC M18 is shown taking part in a Second World War re-enactment event. The mounting of a small-calibre machine gun at the front of the vehicle's turret replicates wartime pictorial evidence of the practice. The M18 has a length of 21ft 10in, a width of 9ft 5in and the vehicle height was 7ft 9in. (*Bob Fleming*)

(*Opposite below*) On display at a historical military rally is a restored M18. Unlike the M10, the M18 had duplicate driver's controls in the front hull meaning that the radioman could also operate the vehicle if called upon. The vehicle had authorized storage for forty-five main gun rounds for its 76mm main gun. Nine of those were in a ready-rack located in the turret. The other thirty-six were stored in the hull crew compartment. (*Christophe Vallier*)

(*Above*) The M18 was, during its time in production, fitted with three different versions of a 76mm main gun labelled as the M1A1, M1A1C and M1A2. The M1A1 and M1A1C were identical except that the latter had threading to accept the fitting of a muzzle brake. When the muzzle brake was not fitted to the M1A1C, it was replaced by a thread protector as seen on the restored M18 pictured here. (*Christophe Vallier*)

(*Opposite above*) This wartime picture shows an M18 with all its authorized external storage in place. The open-topped pannier visible on the front of the turret holds a foul-weather hood for the driver of the vehicle. When required it would fit over the driver's open overhead armoured hatch. There was some late-war effort at developing a roof armoured kit for the M18 but it never went into production. (*TACOM*)

(*Opposite below*) Reflecting the Tank Destroyer Centre's emphasis on mobility over both firepower and protection, the restored M18 pictured here could attain a speed on level roads of 50mph. Wartime experience showed this to have been of little practical value on the battlefield. Rather, its thin armour and lack of a main gun able to deal with late-war German tanks made it fairly useless in its intended role. (*Author's collection*)

(*Above*) The main gun on the restored 90mm GMC M36 pictured here was the only weapon the US army had in the ETO that had the penetrative power to deal with late-war German tanks with some degree of success. The 90mm gun was designated the M3, weighed 2,300lb and had a length of 15ft 5in. The vehicle itself had authorized storage for forty-seven main gun rounds. (*Christophe Vallier*)

(*Opposite above*) Taking part in a Second World War re-enactment event is this privately-owned 90mm GMC M36. The 90mm Gun M3 typically fired an armour-piercing capped projectile labelled the M62. The approximately 24lb projectile portion of the M62 travelled to its intended target at 2,800 feet per second in late production batches. In theory it could penetrate 120mm of armour plate sloped at 30 degrees at a range of 500 yards. (*Bob Fleming*)

(*Opposite below*) In late 1944, the crews of the 90mm GMC M36 in the ETO as shown began receiving small numbers of a new tank-killing round designated as the M304 HVAP (Hyper Velocity Armour Piercing). Instead of steel, the approximately 17lb projectile had a tungsten carbide core. These left the barrel of the 90mm Gun M3 at 3,350 feet per second and in theory could penetrate 221mm of armour at 500 yards. (*National Archives*)

(*Above*) Compared to the 76mm Gun M18, the restored 90mm GMC M36 shown here was not very fast. It had a maximum speed on level roads of 26mph. This made it even slower than the 3-inch GMC M10. The thickest armour on the M36 was the gun shield at 75mm with the turret sides being 32mm thick. The upper front hull (glacis) was 38mm thick and the upper hull sides 25mm thick. (*Christophe Vallier*)

(*Above*) To keep up the production tempo of the 90mm GMC M36 and with the US army running out of a sufficient number of the 3-inch GMC M10 and M10A1 to convert into the M36, the Fisher Tank Arsenal installed the turret of the M36 on the chassis of 187 units of the second-generation M4A3 medium tanks. The US army labelled this vehicle as the 90mm GMC M36B2 and a preserved example is seen here on display. (*Paul Hannah*)

(*Opposite above*) The vehicle commander of this 90mm GMC M36B2 has taken maximum advantage of his surroundings by positioning his vehicle in the alley between two buildings. A factory-designed overhead armoured cover was designed for the open-topped M36. However, pictorial evidence seems to indicate that it did not reach the field before the war in the ETO ended. (*National Archives*)

(*Opposite below*) As an experiment in June 1945 the US army placed the turret from the 90mm GMC M36 onto the chassis of the 76mm GMC M18 as seen in this picture. It was thought that such a vehicle combination would be useful in destroying enemy defensive fortifications during the invasion of mainland Japan. However, the war ended before that project could progress any further and it was soon cancelled. (*TACOM*)

(*Above*) On display is a restored M10C also referred to by the British army as the M10 17-Pounder. As the builders of the 3-inch GMC M10 had had the foresight to design the vehicle's gun shield and mount to accept other weapons, the process of fitting the Lend-Lease-supplied M10s with the 17-pounder gun was not that difficult or time-consuming. (*Christophe Vallier*)

(*Opposite above*) There were some minor modifications required to the American Lend-Lease-supplied 3-inch GMC M10s to re-arm them with the British 17-pounder cannon. These included a new armour casting that was welded to the exterior of the original gun shield as seen in this picture of a restored M10C. This was needed as the barrel of the British gun was smaller in diameter than that of the original American gun. (*Christophe Vallier*)

(*Opposite below*) Visible at almost the end of the barrel of this restored M10C 17-pounder is a counterweight employed to keep the turret balanced as it rotated on uneven surfaces. Just in front of the counterweight is the unique rounded muzzle brake that makes the 17-pounder cannon in all its various versions so easy to identify. (*Chris Hughes*)

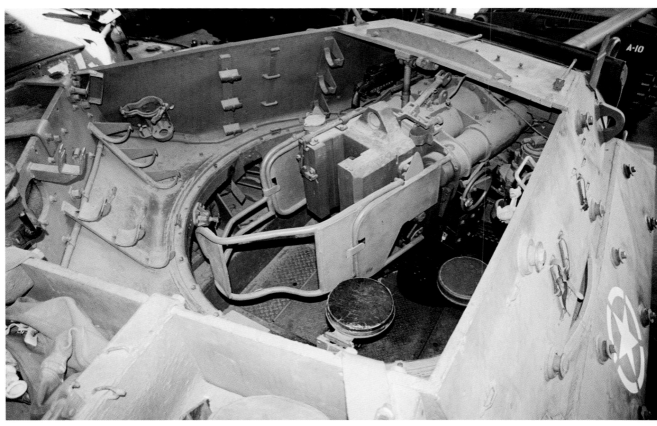

(*Opposite above*) German soldiers look over the turret penetrations that knocked out the M10C seen in this photograph. As the vehicle posed such a threat to German tanks and it was so readily identifiable by its unique rounded muzzle brake and the end of the barrel counterweight, it was often the first target engaged by German tankers. This was an unpleasant fact of life for its crews. (*Tank Museum*)

(*Opposite below*) Pictured is the unrestored turret interior of an M10C. The barrel on the 17-pounder cannon weighed 1,125lb and had a length of just over 14ft. Firing an APCBC (armour-piercing capped ballistic cap) round designated the Mark VIII, its 17lb projectile reached a muzzle velocity of 2,900 feet per second and in theory could penetrate 140mm of armour sloped at 30 degrees at a range of 500 yards. (*Christophe Vallier*)

(*Above*) On display is this preserved example of what the British army labelled as the SP (Self-Propelled) 17-pounder, Valentine Mark I. It was officially named the 'Archer'. The vehicle weighed approximately 37,000lb combat-loaded and is 7ft 4.5in tall, 21ft 11.25in long and 8ft 7.5in wide. (*Vladimir Yakubov*)

The Archer had a maximum armour thickness of 60mm on its front hull. The armoured enclosure for the 17-pounder gun was open-topped, providing only a minimum of protection for the vehicle's gun crew. The maximum speed of the vehicle was 15mph on level ground and only 8mph on uneven terrain. The Archer had authorized main gun ammunition storage for thirty-nine rounds. (*Tank Museum*)

To give their shield-protected towed 2-pounder anti-tank guns improved mobility during the early fighting in North Africa between 1941 and 1942, the British army mounted some of them on the rear cargo beds of available 4 × 4 trucks as shown in this wartime picture. The name applied to this arrangement was 'portee'. (*Tank Museum*)

The Free French army units in North Africa designed and built their own version of an anti-tank gun truck. Upon the rear cargo bed of a British-supplied 4 × 4 Ford truck they mounted a shield-protected 75mm field gun known as the 'Canon de 75 Model 1897' or 'French 75'. In contrast to its Allied counterparts, the French armoured the rear of the truck chassis as seen in this picture. (*Tank Museum*)

On display for many years at the now-closed Military Vehicle Technology Foundation was this restored Australian 2-pounder Anti-tank Gun Carrier. It is 13ft 6in in length and has a width of 6ft 7in. To the top of the vehicle's gun shield it is 6ft 2in tall. During the war years the vehicle was operated by four men: commander, gunner, loader and driver. (*Author's collection*)

(*Opposite above*) Visible in German markings is a captured Red Army SU-85. It was 26ft 9in in length, had a width of 9ft 10in and the vehicle height was 8ft. The 85mm main gun weighed 1,282lb, was 23ft 2in long and originally designed as an anti-aircraft gun. Authorized main gun ammunition storage on the SU-85 was forty-nine rounds. The armour on the front of the vehicle was 45mm thick. (*Bob Fleming*)

(*Opposite below*) German soldiers look over a knocked-out Red Army SU-85. The 85mm main gun on the tank destroyer fired a variety of armour-piercing rounds as well as a high-explosive round. Having entered service in late 1943, it was one of the few vehicles in the Red Army inventory that could destroy German late-war tanks from the front until the T-34-85 medium tank and the IS-2 heavy tank arrived on the scene. (*Bob Fleming*)

(*Above*) The battlefield replacement for the Red Army SU-85 in 1944 was the preserved SU-100 seen here. A number of external spotting features identify the SU-100 when compared to the SU-85. First would be the larger and longer 100mm main gun. Second would be the new vehicle commander's cupola taken from the T-34-85. As with the SU-85, the SU-100 did not have a coaxial machine gun. (*Author's collection*)

Pictured on display is this SU-100. It can be identified as a post-war-built vehicle because it has a large stowage bin fitted on the right front of the hull. Unlike the SU-85, the vehicle commander's position on the SU-100 was extended outward from the right side forward hull due to the larger breech of its main gun. The vehicle had authorized storage for thirty-three main gun rounds. (*Author's collection*)

Despite the front hull plate on the SU-100 being 75mm thick compared to the 45mm on the SU-85 and generally being assigned to over-watch fighting positions, the vehicle could be easily destroyed by the main guns of late-war German tanks as seen in this picture. To compensate for the heavier main gun on the SU-100 and the thicker front armour, the vehicle's front hull suspension components were strengthened. (*Bob Fleming*)

Chapter Three

Self-Propelled Artillery

In the years leading up to the Second World War the US army's Field Artillery Branch showed little interest in the development of self-propelled artillery. It continued to prefer traditional towed artillery, believing that it was more cost-effective and reliable than complex and costly vehicle-mounted artillery. It was also felt that smaller towed artillery pieces would be less noticeable on the battlefield than larger self-propelled artillery pieces.

The Ordnance Branch of the US army had tried prodding the Field Artillery Branch before the Second World War into exploring the possibility of adopting self-propelled artillery but to no avail. It took the outbreak of the war in Europe in 1939 and the birth of the US Armoured Force in July 1940 before the Field Artillery Branch began showing an interest in self-propelled artillery. It had become clear to them by that point in time that towed artillery could not keep up with fast-moving armoured force units.

Stop-Gap SP Artillery

The first example of the Field Artillery Branch's new-found interest in self-propelled artillery was the 105mm HMC (Howitzer Motor Carriage) T19, which entered service in January 1942. It was in production for only four months, with 324 units built by April 1942. The approximately 20,000lb vehicle was based on the modified chassis of the M3 Half-Track Personnel Carrier and mounted the 105mm Howitzer M2A1 in a forward-firing position with limited traverse and elevation.

A problem with the six-man T19 was the fact that the vehicle was not really durable enough to absorb the recoil of the 105mm howitzer. Despite this problem, the T19s were employed during the US army's North African campaign (December 1942 to May 1943). Some of the vehicles would remain in service long enough to be employed by the US army during the invasion of Southern France in August 1944.

105mm SP Artillery

From the beginning the US army wanted a full-tracked self-propelled chassis for the 105mm Howitzer M2A1. The half-track configuration was chosen only in the name of expediency. The US army's replacement for the 105mm HMC T19 was the 105mm

HMC M7 accepted for service in April 1942. The M7 consisted of the 105mm Howitzer M2A1 mounted on the open-topped chassis of the Medium Tank M3.

Production of the approximately 51,000lb M7 began in April 1942 and continued until October 1944 with 2,814 units completed. Besides the US army, the M7 was also employed by the US Marine Corps (USMC) in the Pacific Theatre of Operations (PTO). A total of 832 units of the M7 were provided to the British army under Lend-Lease and they named it the 'Priest'. Some 179 units were also supplied to various other countries under Lend-Lease.

As time went on, the seven-man M7 was improved by incorporating components in its construction from the new M4 series of first-generation medium tanks. Another 826 units of the M7 powered by the Ford GAA engine from the Medium Tank M4A3 came off the assembly line between March 1944 and February 1945. These vehicles were designated as the 105mm HMC M7B1.

Based on the open-topped chassis of the Light Tank M24 was the 105mm HMC M37. Production of the approximately 40,000lb vehicle began in July 1945 with 316 units completed of the seven-man vehicle when production was cancelled at the end of the war. Like the 155mm HMC M41 (see below), the 105mm HMC M37 would also see productive use during the Korean War.

The US army had also explored the mounting of a 105mm Howitzer M3A1 on the open-topped chassis of the Light Tank M5A1 in 1944. The resulting pilot vehicles were designated as the 105mm HMC T82. Testing went well but the end of the war resulted in the project being terminated with no production units completed.

Turreted 105mm SP Artillery

Because the M4 series of medium tanks had been designed with a gun mount that could accommodate different weapons, it was decided to see if the 105mm Howitzer M2A1 could be fitted into the vehicle. Two pilot vehicles based on second-generation M4 series medium tanks armed with a modified version of the 105mm Howitzer M2A1 designated as the M4 soon appeared. Testing of the pilots designated as the M4E5 went well and the US army approved for production two models designated as the M4 (105) and the M4A3 (105).

Between February 1944 and June 1945 a total of 4,680 units of these new five-man howitzer-equipped tanks rolled off the production lines. Broken down further, there were 1,641 units of the approximately M4 (105) built and 3,039 units of the M4A3 (105). Eventually these approximately 73,000lb 105mm howitzer-equipped second-generation M4 series medium tanks would replace the 105mm HMC M7/M7B1 in US army Armoured Divisions. They would provide both direct and indirect fire support missions.

The US army's intended replacement for the M4 (105) and the M4A3 (105) was to have been the Heavy Tank M45 based on the M26 Heavy Tank that had entered into production in November 1944. Production of the five-man M45 armed with the 105mm M4 Howitzer began in July 1945. However, the end of the Second World War resulted in the cancellation of the vehicle with only 185 units having been completed by the end of the year. None would see combat until the Korean War.

In August 1944, the US army recommended the development of a variant of the 76mm GMC M18 armed with a turret-mounted 105mm howitzer. Those pilot vehicles were labelled as the 105mm HMC T88. They were tested with two different models of 105mm howitzers: the T12 and the T51. As with other vehicles developed late in the war, the conclusion of the conflict resulted in the project being cancelled with no production units having been built.

75mm Howitzer SP Artillery

The success of the 105mm HMC T19 led to the production of a similar vehicle beginning in February 1942. It was armed with the 75mm Howitzer M1A1. This vehicle combination was assigned the designation 75mm HMC M3. Production of the five-man vehicle continued until November 1943 with a total of 500 units completed. During the fighting in North Africa, the approximately 20,000lb 75mm HMC M3 performed as an assault gun.

The US army replacement for the 105mm HMC T19 turned out to be the approximately 35,000lb 75mm HMC M8 that was authorized for production in May 1942. The four-man vehicle was based on the modified chassis of the M5 Light Tank and fitted with a newly-designed open-topped turret armed with the 75mm

Howitzer M2 or M3. The first M8 unit rolled off the assembly line in September 1942. Production continued until January 1944, with a total run of 1,778 units completed.

155mm SP Artillery

The US army began studying the possibility of mounting a 155mm gun on the chassis of the Medium Tank M3 in June 1941. The 155mm gun chosen was either French-built and dating from the First World War or an American licence-built copy. These guns were assigned the designation M1917, M1917A1 or M1918M1. The combination of vehicle and gun was approved for production in August 1942 as the 155mm GMC (Gun Motor Carriage) M12.

Between September 1942 and March 1943 a total of 100 units of the approximately 58,000lb M12 were completed. Some seventy-four were later modernized and saw productive use in the ETO between June 1944 and May 1945. Originally employed in the indirect fire of fast-moving armoured units, upon encountering the German Siegfried Line in the autumn of 1944, the six-man M12s proved equally effective in the direct-fire destruction of enemy bunkers.

The success of the M12 in combat and the exhaustion of the supply of 155mm Gun M1917, M1917A1 or M1918M1 led to concept work on a new 155mm self-propelled artillery piece. The chosen replacement for the American licence-built French-designed 155mm gun was the American-designed and built 155mm Gun M1A1 or M2. As the Medium Tank M3 could not support the recoil of the more powerful 155mm gun it was decided to come up with a new chassis using as many components of the second-generation M4 series tanks as possible.

The end result of mating a new 155mm gun and a new open-topped tank-based chassis was designated as the 155mm GMC T83. Testing of the pilot units went well and it was approved for production with 418 units rolling off the assembly line between February 1945 and the end of the year. In May 1945, the eight-man vehicle was redesignated as the 155mm M40. Only a single example would see combat in the ETO before the war ended.

The intended replacement for the 155mm M40 was at one point in time expected to be the 8-inch GMC T93 based on the open-topped chassis of the 90mm Heavy Tank M26. The same chassis was also designed to accept the mounting of the 240mm Howitzer M1, in which case the vehicle would have become the 240mm HMC T92. Only ten pilots of these vehicles were built before they were cancelled upon the end of the war.

155mm Howitzer SP Artillery

Proposed for development in August 1941 was the mounting of the 4.5-inch Gun M1 or the 155mm Howitzer M1 on the open-topped chassis of the Light Tank M5. The pilot vehicles were designated respectively as the 4.5-inch GMC T16 and the 155mm

HMC T64. Testing of the pilots in the summer of 1943 revealed some design issues. As the US army then saw the chassis of the Light Tank M24 as the preferred choice, work on the T16 and T64 came to an end.

Because the US army had also lost interest in the 4.5-inch Gun M1 by the summer of 1943 there would only be the development of the 155mm Howitzer M1 on the open-topped chassis of the Light Tank M24. That five-man vehicle was designated as the 155mm HMC M41. A total of eighty-five were built in 1945 before further production of the vehicle was cancelled. The 42,500lb vehicle did not see combat during the Second World War.

Twenty-four units of the approximately 81,000lb 155mm M40 were eventually re-armed with the 8-inch Howitzer M1 in early 1945. They were labelled as the 8-inch HMC M43. Only a single example would see service in the ETO before the war concluded. A possible replacement for the M43 was the 8-inch HMC T84 based on the chassis of the 90mm Heavy Tank M26. The end of the war resulted in the project being cancelled with only a single pilot completed.

Mortar-Armed Half-Track SP Artillery

Between August 1941 and October 1942, a total of 572 units of the 81mm Mortar Carrier M4 were built for the US army. The six-man vehicle was based on the modified chassis of the M2 Half-Track Car. The original plan called for the onboard mortar to be dismounted before firing, with it being fired from the vehicle only in emergencies. The 81mm carried on board the Mortar Carrier M4 was designated as the M1 and had a maximum range of 3,288 yards. There was authorized storage for ninety-seven rounds of the 81mm mortar ammunition on the Mortar Carrier M4.

Field use of the approximately 17,000lb 81mm Mortar Carrier M4 quickly demon-strated that there was a requirement for the mortar to be fired from the vehicle as standard practice. This resulted in a quick redesign and a new designation as the 81mm Mortar Carrier M4A1, which weighed approximately 18,000lb. A total of 600 units of the M4A1 were built between May and October 1943.

However, the user community was unhappy with the mortar on the M4A1 being fired over the rear of the vehicle. This resulted in the construction of the 81mm Mortar Carrier M21 with a forward-facing mortar. Rather than being based on the chassis of the Half-Track Car M2, the M21 was based on the chassis of the Half-Track Personnel Carrier M3. A total of 110 units of the approximately 20,000lb vehicle were built between January and March 1944.

Some study was done by the US army to see if the 4.2-inch Chemical Mortar could be mounted on the chassis of an armoured half-track. The M3 chassis could not withstand the recoil of the larger mortar. This resulted in the testing of the reinforced chassis of an M3A1 Half-Track Personnel Carrier with the mortar facing rearwards.

That vehicle was designated as the T21 and another version with the mortar facing forward as the T21E. Neither vehicle was ordered into production.

Mortar-Armed Full-Track SP Artillery

In 1941 the British army ordered a version of the Universal Carrier designated as the 3-inch Mortar Carrier Mark II. The mortar was stored on the vehicle disassembled and when brought into action was removed from the vehicle and assembled for firing by the three-man crew. Sixty-six rounds of ammunition for the mortar were carried on board the vehicle and would consist of both high-explosive and smoke.

In late 1943, the US army embarked upon the development of a tank-based mortar-armed vehicle. It consisted of the turretless chassis of the Light Tank M5A1 armed with the 81mm Mortar M1. The vehicle combination was designated as the 81mm MMC (Mortar Motor Carriage) T27. It was later decided to replace the 81mm Mortar M1 on the turretless M5A1 with the 4.2-inch Mortar M2. This resulted in the label 4.2-inch Mortar Carrier T29. Neither vehicle was ordered into production.

In January 1945, the US army began looking at the concept of fitting the 155mm Mortar T9 into the turret of an M4 series medium tank. The resulting vehicle was to be referred to as the 155mm MMC T90. Only a mock-up of the T90 had been completed by the time the war ended and the project was soon cancelled.

The British army had as an experiment mounted a British-designed and built 9.75-inch mortar on two redundant examples of de-gunned 105mm HMC M7 Priests in early 1945, but this was never ordered into production. At the same time, the US army decided to go forward with a self-propelled motor project. The resulting vehicle was designated as the 250mm MMC T94. It was still in development when the war ended and the project was quickly cancelled.

In May 1945, the month in which the Germans formally surrendered, the US army initialled the development of a new full-tracked mortar vehicle. It involved mounting the 4.2-inch Mortar M2 on the de-gunned chassis of the 105mm HMC M37. Only a pilot was built before the project was cancelled.

SP Rocket Artillery

In addition to conventional tubed artillery, the US army introduced into service during the latter part of the Second World War a small number of the Rocket Launcher T34. It was an add-on field kit with sixty plastic tubes, each of which was loaded with a 4.5-inch (114mm) M8 Rocket fitted with an HE warhead.

The add-on rocket kit was intended for attachment to the turrets of first-generation M4 series medium tanks and aimed and fired from within the safety of the vehicles. The T34 was nicknamed the 'Calliope' due to its overall resemblance to an old-fashioned steam-powered pipe organ. It did not prove popular in the field with the tankers who had to deal with it and the T34 only saw very limited service.

SP Half-Track Anti-Aircraft Vehicles

The US army was very impressed by the German army's early-war employment of close air support. The anticipation of encountering German ground-attack aircraft on future battlefields led the US army to develop and field self-propelled anti-aircraft vehicles.

During the Second World War anti-aircraft guns could be fixed, towed or self-propelled with all being referred to as 'Anti-aircraft Artillery' by the US army and considered part of the artillery branch of the service.

The first self-propelled anti-aircraft vehicle taken into service by the US army was labelled the Multiple GMC M13. It consisted of a modified M3 Half-Track Personnel Carrier fitted with a one-man powered armoured turret in its rear hull compartment armed with two air-cooled Browning .50 machine guns, M2HB. The turret was designated as the Twin .50 Calibre Machine-Gun Mount M33. A total of 1,103 units of the Multiple GMC M13 were built between January and May 1943.

The US army's replacement for the five-man Multiple GMC M13 was the five-man Multiple GMC M16. Rather than the two air-cooled Browning .50 machine guns M2HB, it was armed with four. The powered gun mount in the rear hull compartment of the vehicle was labelled as the Quad .50 Calibre Machine-Gun Mount M45. As with the one-man powered armoured turret in the Multiple GMC M13, that mounted in the Multiple GMC M16 was designed and built by the W.L. Maxson Corporation.

Production of the approximately 20,000lb M16 began in December 1942 and continued until March 1944 with 3,614 units assembled. There was also an improvised version of the vehicle referred to as M16B. A total of 332 units were constructed in England prior to D-Day on 6 June 1944 to make up for a perceived shortage of the M16 among the US army units assigned to the invasion force.

Lend-Lease SP Half-Track Anti-Aircraft Vehicles

The Twin .50 Calibre Machine-Gun Mount M33 was also fitted to the modified M5 Half-Track Personnel Carrier. In this guise it became the Multiple GMC M14, of which 1,805 units were built between December 1942 and December 1943. All were allocated to Lend-Lease with most being stripped of their machine-gun power-operated turrets and converted for other roles by the British and Commonwealth armies that received them.

The Quad .50 Calibre Machine-Gun Mount M45 was also installed in the rear hull compartment of a modified M5 Half-Track Personnel Carrier, resulting in the designation Multiple GMC M17. A total of 1,000 units of the approximately 20,000lb vehicle were constructed between December 1943 and March 1944. As with the Multiple GMC M14, all were allocated to Lend-Lease and these were shipped to the Soviet Union for use by the Red Army.

Dual-Purpose SP Anti-Aircraft Half-Tracks

In the summer of 1942, the US army identified a requirement for a self-propelled anti-aircraft vehicle with weapons also able to engage enemy tanks. Upon a modified Half-Track Personnel Carrier M3 they mounted a combination gun mount armed with a single 37mm Anti-aircraft Gun M1A2 and two Browning .50 M2 water-cooled machine guns. The seven-man vehicle was designated as the Multiple GMC T28.

A total of eighty units of the Multiple GMC T28 were constructed and the vehicles saw useful service with the US army during the North African campaign in the anti-aircraft role. Impressed by the T28, the US army decided that it wanted an upgraded version that became the Multiple GMC M15. A total of 2,252 units of the M15 and a modified version of the vehicle labelled as the Combination GMC M15A1 were built between February 1943 and February 1944. The seven-man M15A1 weighed approximately 21,000lb.

Rejected Anti-Aircraft Vehicles

There were a number of anti-aircraft weapon configurations tested on the modified chassis of various half-tracks. These included two air-cooled 20mm Mark IV Oerlikon guns fitted to the M45 powered-operated turret of the Multiple GMC M16 in lieu of four machine guns. That vehicle was labelled as the Twin 20mm GMC T10E1. It was approved for production with 110 units built in March 1944 before the programme was cancelled with none seeing combat.

The US army also tested the possibility of mounting an anti-aircraft turret armed with four large-calibre air-cooled machine guns on the chassis of the Light Armoured Car M8. The pilot was designated as the Multiple GMC T69. Testing of the vehicle led the US army to conclude that its existing half-track-based machine-gun-armed anti-aircraft vehicles were superior and the T69 project was terminated.

Tank-Based Gun-Armed Anti-Aircraft Vehicles

In October 1941, the US army considered mounting a low-velocity 75mm anti-aircraft gun on the modified chassis of the Medium Tank M3, which could do double duty as an anti-tank weapon. By March 1942 work on the project was terminated as it was clear that the chosen 75mm gun was ineffective, both as an anti-aircraft and an anti-tank gun.

Next up was the 40mm Automatic Gun M1 mounted on the chassis of the Medium Tank M3. This vehicle was designated as the 40mm GMC T36. A follow-on vehicle was the Multiple GMC T52 that was also armed with the 40mm Automatic Gun M1 but with the addition of two large-calibre air-cooled machine guns. It was mounted on the chassis of the Medium Tank M4A2. Both the T36 and T37 would be cancelled due to a host of design issues such as having insufficient onboard ammunition storage space.

The US army also began work in June 1942 on the mounting of the 90mm Guns M1 on the chassis of the Medium Tank M4 series, which was thought could do double duty as an anti-tank gun. The first iteration of the vehicle was designated as the 90mm GMC T53. Test results led to the construction of a second and third pilot labelled as the 90mm GMC T53E1. The project was eventually cancelled due to lack of onboard ammunition storage space and a host of other design issues.

The Canadian army had also explored the concept of mounting a large-calibre anti-aircraft gun on a redundant medium tank chassis. Rather than employing the American-designed and built 90mm Gun M1, they used the British army equivalent designated as the Ordnance, QF, 3.7-inch (94mm) Anti-aircraft Gun. However, the Canadian army experiment was plagued by the same design issues that had hampered the US army's efforts and was soon cancelled.

Light Tank-Based Anti-Aircraft Vehicles

Some developmental work was done on fitting the open-topped chassis of a modified Light Tank M5 with powered gun mounts armed with either four or two 20mm guns. These were labelled respectively as the Multiple 20mm Gun Mounts T19 and T19E1. Both were cancelled in October 1943 to be replaced by another anti-aircraft concept vehicle in early 1945 based on the Light Tank M5 and designated the 20mm GMC T85E1.

By this time the 20mm GMC T85E1 pilot was ready for testing. The US army decided that it preferred to see twin 40mm Gun M1s mounted on the Light Tank M5 chassis. This resulted in a vehicle designated as the 40mm GMC T65. As the Light Tank M5 was then being replaced by the Light Tank M24, the US army switched gears again and they wanted to use the modified chassis of the Light Tank M24 to mount twin 40mm M1 Guns rather than the chassis of the Light Tank M5.

The M24-based anti-aircraft vehicle became the Twin 40mm GMC M19. The six-man vehicle had been approved for production in June 1944. However, production did not begin until April 1945. Only 300 units were built before the order was cancelled, with none of the M19s seeing combat during the Second World War.

Tank-Based Machine-Gun-Armed Anti-Aircraft Vehicles

Unhappy with the poor off-road mobility of its machine-gun-armed half-track-based anti-aircraft vehicles, the US army experimented with a number of tank-based machine-gun-armed anti-aircraft alternatives. The first pilot was tested with the Quad .50 Calibre Machine Gun Mount M45 placed on the chassis of a turretless Light Tank M3. That had not progressed very far when the US army decided in July 1943 that the newly-designed chassis of the Light Tank M24 would be a better choice.

The vehicle that evolved from the US army decision to use the Light Tank M24 chassis was designated as the Multiple GMC T77. Rather than using the one-man Quad .50 Calibre Machine Gun Mount M45, a new enclosed two-man turret referred to as the T89 and armed with six large-calibre air-cooled machine guns was developed. The first pilot of the T77 was completed in July 1945, with an improved model designated as the T77E1 fitted with a more advanced fire-control system. Neither was placed into production.

British Army SP Artillery

The only self-propelled artillery piece to come out of British industry during the Second World War was named the 'Bishop'. It consisted of the British-designed and built Ordnance, QF, 25-pounder (83mm) gun/howitzer mounted on the modified chassis of the British army Valentine tank. The weapon was fitted inside a slab-sided armoured enclosure on the top of the vehicle's hull. The vehicle's official designation was Carrier, Valentine, 25-pounder Gun Mark I Bishop. The approximately 39,000lb vehicle had a crew of four men.

The first batch of Bishops ordered in November 1941 was for 100 vehicles. The American Lend-Lease-supplied 105mm HMC M7 Priest proved far superior, and the order for additional units of the Bishop was cancelled, only to be rescinded in July 1942 with an order for fifty further units. The Bishops would see combat during the North African campaign on to Sicily and Italy before being pulled from front-line service in late 1943. Post-1943 the Bishops were retained for training purposes only.

Canadian Army Input

The 105mm HMC M7 Priest supplied to the British army under Lend-Lease was considered a first-rate vehicle. The problem was that the 105mm M2A1 Howitzer with which it was armed was not standard equipment for the British army. In June 1942, American industry began a project to see if the M7 Priest could be modified to be armed with the British-designed and built 25-pounder gun. The pilot vehicle for that project was assigned the designation 25-pounder GMC T51.

Further work on the 25-pounder GMC T51 project was cancelled in March 1943 as the British army now preferred a Canadian solution to their requirement. That involved mounting a Canadian licence-built copy of the 25-pounder gun on the redundant chassis of the Canadian-built Ram II Cruiser Tank. It would be named the 'Ram 25-pdr' and later as the 'Sexton I'. A total of 124 units was ordered by the Canadian army and were built between April and September 1943.

The British army was very impressed with the Sexton I and contracted with Canadian industry to build a similar version on the redundant chassis of the Canadian Grizzly tank, while still using components from the Ram II Cruiser Tank. This version of the vehicle became known as the 'Sexton II'. All told, 2,065 units of the six-man vehicle were built for the British and other Commonwealth armies by early 1944. The Polish army units fighting with the Western Allies were also supplied with the approximately 57,000lb Sexton II.

The Canadian army anticipated a requirement in 1943 for a tank-based anti-aircraft platform to support its armoured units during the planned invasion of France in 1944. Canadian industry therefore came up with an armoured turret fitted with four 20mm Polsten guns. That turret was designed to fit on the redundant chassis of Canadian Grizzly tanks with vehicles so equipped being named the 'Skink'. Only three production units of the vehicle and eight spare turrets were built before the project was cancelled in early 1944.

Howitzer-Armed Tanks

The British army did field tanks fitted with howitzers instead of guns during the Second World War and assigned them the acronym 'CS' (Close Support). They were intended only for the direct-fire role. The first was the Churchill Infantry Tank, labelled as the 'Churchill I'. It was armed with a turret-mounted 2-pounder gun and a front hull-mounted Ordnance, QF, 3-inch Howitzer. A later version had the 3-inch howitzer in the turret and the 2-pounder cannon in the front hull.

Out of approximately 950 units of the Centaur Cruiser Tank series built, eighty units were armed with the Ordnance, QF, 95mm Howitzer in lieu of the standard 6-pounder gun. These vehicles were designated as the Centaur IV and employed by the Royal Marine Armoured Support Group on D-Day (6 June 1944, the invasion of France) for dealing with German defensive fortifications and for the two weeks thereafter before being withdrawn from service.

The same 95mm howitzer that went into the Centaur IV also went into 341 units of the Cromwell Cruiser tank labelled the Mark VI. In addition, the 95mm howitzer armed an unknown number of the Mark VIII version of the Churchill Infantry Tank. The weapon was capable of firing a variety of rounds including HE, smoke and an HEAT (high-explosive anti-tank) round.

SP Anti-Aircraft Vehicles

During the Battle for France, in the summer of 1940, the British army was very impressed by the German employment of ground-attack aircraft in support of their armoured units. To deal with this future threat the British army set out to develop a series of self-propelled anti-aircraft vehicles based on the chassis of existing tracked and wheeled vehicles.

The first self-propelled anti-aircraft vehicle was designated the Tank, Light AA Mark I and armed with four 7.92mm BESA turret-mounted machine guns. It was quickly replaced by an upgraded version labelled as Tank, Light AA Mark II, which retained the same turret-mounted armament of the earlier model. The turret mounted on the Tank, Light AA Mark II was also fitted onto a 4 × 4 armoured car designated as the Humber AA Mark I, 1942.

The light tank series on which the Tank, Light AA Mark II and Tank Light AA Mark II were based were pulled from front-line service by 1942. The British army went on to develop and field anti-aircraft vehicles on the next generation of tanks, which was the Crusader series that first saw combat in North Africa in June 1941.

There were two anti-aircraft versions of the Crusader tank built. The first was the Crusader II, AA Mark I armed with a 40mm gun protected by a gun shield. Second was the Crusader III, AA Mark II armed with two turret-mounted 20mm guns. The turret from the Crusader III, AA Mark II was later fitted to the Centaur tank chassis and became the Centaur AA Mark II.

The turret from the Crusader III, AA Mark II was also fitted to a 4 × 4 armoured car and labelled as the AEC AA 1943. In addition, there was an improvised anti-aircraft version of the Crusader tank armed with three 20mm guns on an unarmoured mount.

In early 1943 the British army requested that an anti-aircraft version of the American-designed and built Armoured Car T17E1, which they had named the 'Staghound,' be designed and built. American industry therefore mounted a turret armed with two air-cooled Browning .50 calibre M2HB machine guns onto the hull of a modified T17E1. That vehicle was designated as the Armoured Car T17E2.

A total of 1,000 units of the approximately 27,000lb Armoured Car T17E2 were built between October 1943 and April 1944. All were delivered to the British army under Lend-Lease. In British army service it was known as the 'Staghound AA'.

Red Army SP Artillery

Pre-German Invasion

The Red Army had decided in the early 1930s that it needed self-propelled guns/howitzers and its artillery branch subsequently came up with prototype models of varying sizes and armament. The only one accepted into production prior to the Second World War was a variant of the BT-7 series of light tanks, designated the BT-7 artillery or BT-7 with 76mm howitzer in an oversized turret.

A total of 154 units of the BT-7A were built between 1936 and 1938; however, only 134 units were eventually fielded. All would be lost during the initial phase of the German invasion of the Soviet Union that began in June 1941.

During the Russo-Finnish War (1939–40) the Red Army identified a need for a howitzer-armed tank with a large enough weapon to destroy the reinforced Finnish army bunkers being encountered. It was decided to mount a newly-designed turret armed with a 152mm L/20 howitzer on the chassis of the new KV-1 Heavy Tank. Production of the vehicle labelled as the KV with big turret or KV-2 began in July 1940. A total of 204 units of the vehicle were built with almost all being destroyed in the early stages of the German invasion.

Post-German Invasion

Following the terrible losses of tanks sustained by the Red Army in 1941, what resources it could amass were dedicated to replacing them as quickly as possible. There was little industrial capacity remaining at the time to design and build specialized vehicles such as self-propelled guns or howitzers. Nevertheless, by the spring of 1942 the Red Army recognized a pressing need for them to deal with enemy defensive positions.

The first self-propelled artillery piece to enter the Red Army inventory following the German invasion was the approximately 23,000lb SU-76 Light Self-Propelled Gun. It was quickly superseded in production by an improved model designated as the SU-76M. Both models consisted of the lengthened chassis of the T-70 light tank upon which a ZiS-3 76.2mm field gun was mounted.

The 76.2mm field gun on the SU-76 series was mounted at the rear of the vehicle's hull in an armoured open-topped compartment. The weapon was serviced by a crew of three and had limited elevation and traverse. The weapon was capable of both direct and indirect fire as were all Red Army self-propelled guns. Between the summer of 1942 and 1945 a total of 14,292 units were built with 13,932 being the SU-76M.

Improvised SP Artillery

In early 1943 the Red Army gave approval for conversion of some of its inventory of captured German Panzer III medium tanks into turretless self-propelled artillery pieces. They were to be armed with a version of the 76.2mm tank gun mounted in the first-generation T-34 series tanks. These ad hoc vehicles were designated as the SU-76i Light Self-Propelled gun. The suffix 'i' is the abbreviation for the Russian word *inostrrannaya*, meaning foreign.

Unlike the SU-76 series, the SU-76i had an armoured roof for the gun crew. A total of 201 units of the SU-76i were built between March and November 1943. However, they would only last in service for about a year before the supply of spare parts for the Panzer III chassis was exhausted. In addition to the SU-76i there was the SG-122. This consisted of a Red Army 122mm howitzer M-30 mounted on the turretless chassis of twenty-one captured German Panzer III medium tanks.

Late-War SP Artillery

On the heels of the SU-76 series, the Red Army gave approval in October 1942 for the development of another self-propelled artillery piece designated as the SU-122. The turretless vehicle consisted of the chassis of the T-34 series Medium Tank armed with an M-30S 122mm howitzer fitted inside an armoured casemate. Production of the SU-122 began in December 1942 and continued until the middle of 1943 with 638 units of the approximately 66,000lb vehicle built.

In the Red Army all artillery pieces had a secondary role as anti-tank weapons. The poor anti-tank performance of the howitzer in the SU-122 had led to the vehicle's early cancellation. Its replacement would be the turretless SU-152, which entered service in May 1943. The approximately 100,000lb vehicle consisted of the chassis of the KV-1S Heavy Tank armed with the ML-20 152mm howitzer in an armoured casemate. Only 670 units of the SU-152 were built before production concluded in Janary 1944.

Because production of the KV-1S Heavy Tank was ordered to be halted in August 1943 in favour of the new IS-2 Heavy Tank, it was decided to come up with an updated version of the SU-152 on the new heavy tank chassis. It was assigned the designation ISU-152 and weighed approximately 101,000lb. The ISU-152 was armed with the same weapon as the SU-152.

The armoured casemate on the ISU-152 could also be armed with a 122mm field gun labelled as the A19S. In this configuration the vehicle became the ISU-122. An improved 122mm howitzer referred to as the D-25S fitted to the ISU-122 resulted in the vehicle designation ISU-122S. Unlike the ISU-122, the howitzer fitted to the ISU-122S had a semi-automatic breech, large muzzle brake and a smaller gun shield.

Production of the ISU-152 and the ISU-122 began in late 1943. At the conclusion of the Second World War a total of 1,885 units of the ISU-152 had been built and 1,435 units of the ISU-122. There were also 475 units of the ISU-122S assembled. The ISU-122 and ISU-122S were preferred for engaging enemy tanks at longer range when they appeared and the ISU-152 for dealing with enemy fortifications due to its much larger HE round.

(*Opposite above*) Pictured is the pilot of the 105mm HMC T19. To compensate for the added weight of the 105mm M2A1 howitzer its original mount was redesigned to spread its weight over a greater area of the vehicle. In addition, the frame of the T19 was strengthened as testing revealed that it would sag when subjected to off-road conditions. (*TACOM*)

(*Opposite below*) The pilot of the 105mm HMC T19 is seen here being tested at the US army's Desert Training Centre. The production examples were fitted with an armoured shield to protect the gun crew. As the blast from the firing of the vehicle's weapons damaged the front headlights of the pilot, the production units were provided with dismountable headlights. (*TACOM*)

Shown is one of the two pilots built of the 75mm HMC T30 with its weapon at maximum elevation. The 75mm M1A1 howitzer mounted in the T30 had a rate of fire of six rounds per minute. Maximum range of the rounds was 9,760 yards. Of the 500 units ordered, only 312 were configured as the T30 with the remainder being converted back to the Half-Track Personnel Carrier M3. (TACOM)

The replacement for the 75mm HMC T30 was the 75mm HMC M8 seen here based on the chassis of the Light Tank M5. Due to the increased size of the vehicle's open-topped turret, the overhead hatches for the driver and assistant were eliminated on the M8. Both crewmen entered and left their front hull positions by way of the turret. (TACOM)

Note the two large vision ports in the front hull of this restored 75mm HMC M8. Both front hull crewmen on the M8 also had two rotating overhead periscopes that are also visible in this image. As the M8 had dual controls, the vehicle could be operated by either front hull crewman. The M8 was armed with either the 75mm Howitzer M2 or M3. (*TACOM*)

The 75mm HMC M8 seen here in action was originally intended to serve as an assault gun for light tank battalions. However, as these types of units were very uncommon by the time they reached field units in the summer of 1944, the M8s were typically assigned to provide fire support for US army cavalry reconnaissance squadrons. (*Patton Museum*)

The half-track-based 105mm HMC T19 was an interim vehicle awaiting the US army's development of a full-tracked counterpart. Pictured is the pilot vehicle intended to fill that role designated as the 105mm HMC T32. It was based on the open-topped chassis of the Medium Tank M3. Testing of the pilot went well and it was ordered into production with some design modifications as the 105mm HMC M7. (TACOM)

Pictured is an early-production example of the 105mm HMC M7, which can be identified by the location of its upper return roller. The design changes introduced between the pilot 105mm HMC T32 and the production 105mm HMC M7 included raising the front armour hull (superstructure) and the addition of an anti-aircraft mount on the right forward superstructure of the vehicle. (TACOM)

A posed wartime photograph of a 105mm HMC M7. It can be identified as an early-production unit because it lacks the hinged armour plates along the sides and rear of the fighting compartment. These were added to later-production units of the M7 because the vertically-stored 105mm rounds were partially exposed above the superstructure on earlier production units. *(Patton Museum)*

On display is this preserved 105mm HMC M7. It is a later production unit as the vehicle's return rollers are now set back from the bogie assemblies and it has the hinged armour plates along the visible side of the vehicle's superstructure. The M7 driver was provided with a direct vision port that could be covered by an armoured hatch fitted with a periscope as seen in this picture. *(Christophe Vallier)*

In this posed wartime photograph of a 105mm HMC M7 we see what appears to be the smoke emanating from the barrel of the vehicle's weapon upon firing. The M7 series would appear with both the single-piece differential and final drive housing as pictured, as well as the three-piece differential and final drive housing inherited from the Medium Tank M3. (*Patton Museum*)

Belonging to a private collector is this restored 105mm HMC M7 fitted with its canvas foul-weather covering. The M7 had authorized storage space for sixty-nine rounds of 105mm ammunition in its fighting compartment. As with the 105mm HMC T19, the M7 was armed with a 105mm Howitzer M2A1. (*Author's collection*)

The US army desired a lighter-weight full-tracked vehicle armed with a 105mm howitzer to replace the 105mm HMC M7. That vehicle turned out to be the 105mm HMC M37 seen here on display. The 105mm howitzer mounted in the M37 was originally designed for mounting in the turret of the Medium Tank M4 and was labelled as the 105mm Howitzer M4. (*Paul Hannah*)

Visible in this picture is the interior of a restored 105mm HMC M37. The vehicle has authorized storage space for 126 rounds of 105mm ammunition. Unlike the 105mm rounds in the M7 that were stored vertically in individual bins, the 105mm rounds in the M37 were stored horizontally in two large separate bins on either side of the fighting compartment as seen in this picture. (*Chris Hughes*)

In the US army's search for an ever lighter and smaller full-tracked vehicle able to mount a 105mm howitzer, the 105mm HMC T82 seen here was constructed. The short-barrelled 105mm howitzer mounted in the vehicle was originally designed as a towed weapon for use by airborne units and designated as the 105mm Howitzer M3. (TACOM)

Pictured is a restored example of an early-production example of the M4(105) riding on a Vertical Volute Spring Suspension (VVSS) system. The power traverse system found on the standard gun-armed M4 series medium tanks was not fitted to speed up production. There was authorized storage space for sixty-six rounds on the vehicle. (Pierre-Olivier Buan)

Shown is an M4A3(105) riding on the second-generation Horizontal Volute Spring Suspension (HVSS) system. The omission of a powered turret-traverse system for the 105mm howitzer-armed M4 series medium tanks was a serious mistake. This was soon corrected on the production line but none fitted with a powered turret-traverse system reached the field before the war ended. *(Pierre-Olivier Buan)*

The M45 Heavy Tank pictured here during the Korean War was armed with the 105mm Howitzer M4. It had authorized storage for seventy-four rounds and came off the production line with a powered turret-traverse system. Post-war, the vehicle was reclassified as the Medium Tank M45. The gun shield on the M45 was 8in thick and the front hull (glacis) 5in thick. *(Patton Museum)*

In this picture we see the pilot 155mm GMC T6 in its original configuration in February 1942. The T6 was based on the much-modified chassis of redundant Medium Tanks M3 and was eventually designated as the 155mm GMC M12. The 155mm gun fitted to the vehicle was of French design dating from the First World War. (*Patton Museum*)

This wartime photograph shows a 155mm GMC M12 being employed in the direct-fire mode. There was authorized storage on the vehicle for twenty projectiles and an equal number of propelling charges. To support the M12 in the field, another modified version of the Medium Tank M3 was configured to carry additional ammunition. It was labelled as the Cargo Carrier M30. (*Patton Museum*)

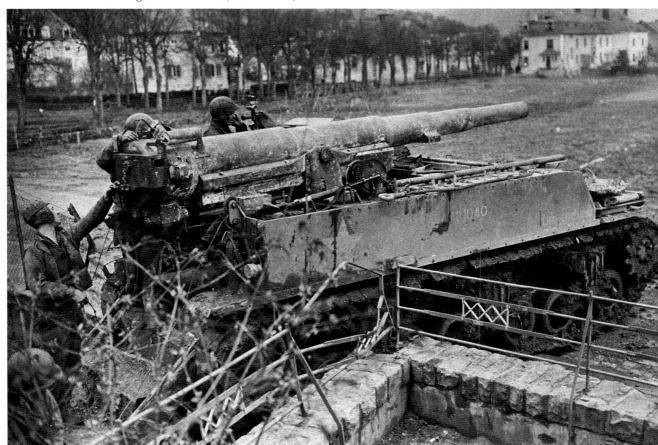

Shown in its firing position is the sole example of the 8-inch GMC T93. In general configuration it matched that of its predecessors, the 155mm GMC M12 and the 155mm GMC M40. There was a large spade at the rear of the hull intended to absorb recoil. On the top of the spade was a hinged platform for use by the gun crew when it was lowered. *(TACOM)*

(*Above*) A preserved example of the 155mm GMC M40 is seen here at a US army museum. The 155mm gun mounted on the M40 was designated as either the M1A1 or M2 and has a barrel length of 22ft 9in. The projectile portion of the HE round fired by the weapon weighed approximately 95lb and the separate-loading propelling charge about 32lb. (*Paul Hannah*)

(*Opposite above*) On display at an American military museum is a 155mm HMC M41. Based on a much-modified chassis of the Light Tank M24, the vehicle is armed with the 155mm Howitzer M1. Work on the weapon had begun in 1942 and by the time the Second World War had concluded over 6,000 units had been built with the majority being fitted to towed carriages. (*Christophe Vallier*)

(*Opposite below*) Using the chassis of the 155mm GMC M40 with some minor change in ammunition storage arrangements is this preserved vehicle designated as the 8-inch HMC M43. The weapon fired an HE projectile that weighed 200lb. The propelling charge for the separate-loading projectile weighed 29.6lb. Maximum range of the howitzer was 2,140 yards. (*Author's collection*)

Based on the Half-Track Car M2 was the Half-Track 81mm Mortar Carrier M4 seen here. A US army mortar platoon leader in the ETO commented in a March 1945 report: 'It is my opinion that our own 81mm mortar is as good as the German 81mm mortar for infantry work. But in regards to it being used for armor support I firmly believe the German 120mm mortar would fill the bill a great deal better.' (*TACOM*)

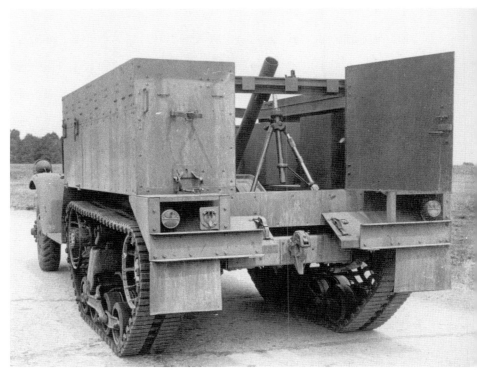

Visible in this Half-Track 81mm Mortar Carrier M4A1 is the traversing fixture under the mortar bipod legs on the vehicle's floor. This feature was lacking on the previous Half-Track 81mm Mortar Carrier M4A1 and hence greatly restricted its arc of traverse, which was hemmed in by mortar ammunition bins not seen on the M4A1. (*TACOM*)

As the user community had decided early on that the most efficient location of an 81mm Mortar M1 in a half-track was in a forward-firing position, the US army therefore fielded the Half-Track 81mm Mortar Carrier M21 seen here. It was based on the chassis of the Half-Track Personnel Carrier M3. The normal rate of fire for the 81mm Mortar M1 was eighteen rounds per minute. *(Patton Museum)*

Beginning in March 1945, the US army began exploring the concept of mounting the 10-inch Mortar T5E2 on the chassis of the 155mm GMC M40. The resulting pilot vehicle pictured was fitted with a wooden mock-up of the 10-inch mortar and designated as the 250mm MMC T94. Upon the end of the war the US army lost interest and further work on the project was cancelled in 1946. *(TACOM)*

A heavily-sandbagged first-generation M4 series medium tank in the ETO is shown here fitted with the Rocket Launcher T34, which weighed 1,840lb. The 90in-long plastic launcher tubes that formed part of the T34 were arranged with a double bank of thirty-six on top and two double banks of twelve below. Upon the last rocket being expended, the entire T34 assembly could be jettisoned. (*Patton Museum*)

The Rocket Launcher T34 seen here in action fired the 4.5-inch HE Rocket M8 series. The same rockets could also be fired from aerial platforms. The rockets themselves could vary in weight between 14 and 16lb and contained 4.3lb of HE filler. The M8 rocket series had a length of approximately 31in. Maximum range of the rockets was 4,000 yards. (*Patton Museum*)

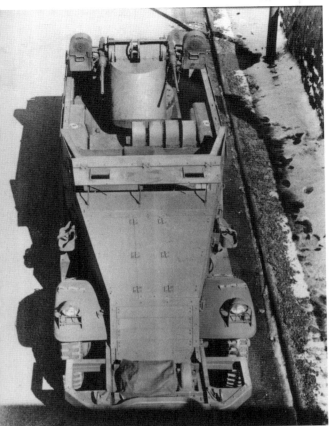

The US army's initial reaction to the threat of German ground-attack aircraft was to see if a modified twin machine-gun-armed powered turret developed for aircraft could be mounted on a suitable wheeled vehicle. Testing soon revealed that only half-tracks were heavy and large enough to provide a stable firing platform. This led to the adoption of the Multiple GMC M13 seen here. (*Patton Museum*)

As the twin machine-gun-armed powered turret in the Multiple GMC M13 proved both reliable and easy to maintain, the US army quickly asked for the production of a near-identical powered turret armed with four large-calibre air-cooled machine guns. Vehicles so equipped were designated the Multiple GMC M16 with a restored example pictured here.

(*Author's collection*)

The quad machine-gun-armed turret seen here on this restored Multiple GMC M16 was labelled as the Multiple Calibre .50 Machine Gun Mount M45. The M16 had authorized storage for 5,000 rounds of large-calibre machine-gun ammunition. The folding armour panels on the sides and rear of the vehicle's armoured superstructure increased the maximum depression of the onboard weapons. *(Pierre-Olivier Buan)*

The owner of this Half-Track Personnel Carrier M3 has recreated an improvised wartime US army vehicle unofficially referred to as the M16B. He has done this by mounting a Multiple Calibre .50 Machine Gun Mount M45 on his vehicle. His recreation and the wartime examples, also mounted on the Half-Track Car M2, could be identified by the lack of the folding armour panels that appeared on the factory-built Multiple GMC M16 units. *(Pierre-Olivier Buan)*

Shown here is the first production unit of the Half-Track Multiple GMC T28. The 37mm Gun M1A2 that formed part of the vehicle's armament fired an HE round that had a maximum vertical ceiling of 18,600ft. The two water-cooled M2 .50 calibre machine guns on the T28 had a rate of fire of 500 to 650 rounds per minute. (TACOM)

The replacement for the Half-Track Multiple GMC T28 was the Multiple GMC M15. Unlike on the earlier vehicle, the M15 gun crew was provided with a three-sided armoured shield as shown in this picture of the pilot. The two water-cooled M2 .50 calibre machine guns of the T28 were replaced on the M15 by two air-cooled M2 HB .50 calibre machine guns. (TACOM)

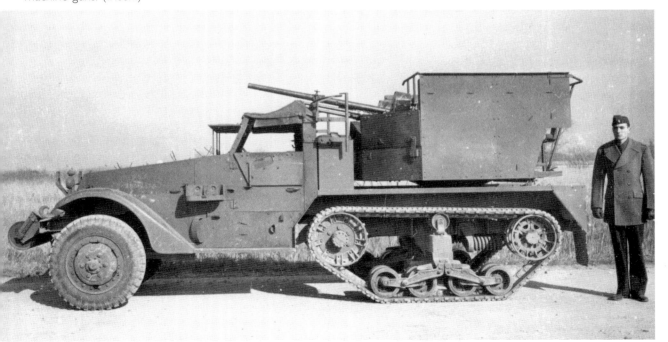

(*Above*) In this photograph we can see a 37mm Gun M1A2 being loaded. It formed part of what was designated as the Combination Gun Mount M42 mounted on the rear of the Combination GMC Carriage M15A1. It can be identified as such by the fact that the two air-cooled M2 .50 calibre machine guns are located below the 37mm Gun M1A2. On the earlier Multiple GMC M15 gun mount they are located above the 37mm gun. (*TACOM*)

(*Opposite above*) In an effort to field self-propelled anti-aircraft vehicles able to engage attacking aircraft with larger and more powerful rounds, the US army experimented with a vehicle seen here that was designated as the Half-Track Multiple GMC T10. It was armed with two 20mm automatic guns. Problems with the T10 led to the redesigned T10E1. Production of the T10E1 was authorized but ended due to ammunition design issues. (*TACOM*)

(*Opposite below*) There was a US army experiment that involved mounting a large armoured shield-protected gun mount on the lengthened chassis of an M2 Half-Track Car as pictured here. The gun mount was armed with four 20mm Mark IV Oerlikon anti-aircraft guns and two air-cooled M2 .50 Machine Guns. Tests quickly revealed that the half-track chassis could not support the weight of the gun mount and the project was terminated. (*Patton Museum*)

288541

(*Opposite above*) Experiments were conducted to see if the 40mm Automatic Gun M1 in either a single or twin gun mount could be fitted onto the modified chassis of M3 Half-Track Personnel Carriers. Those projects were eventually cancelled as the vehicles could not support the weight of the gun mounts or recoil. By this time the US army preferred a full-tracked anti-aircraft vehicle. (*Patton Museum*)

(*Opposite below*) A US army ordnance unit based in Australia removed the Combination Gun Mount M42 from eighteen units of the Multiple GMC M15. They replaced it with a locally-built mount armed with a single 40mm Automatic Gun M1, which was protected by a four-sided armoured shield. One of those improvised vehicles is shown here and was unofficially referred to as the 'M15 Special'. (*Patton Museum*)

(*Above*) Pictured here is the single pilot of the 40mm GMC T36 with its main armament at maximum elevation. The vehicle consisted of the much-modified hull of a Medium Tank M3 upon which was fitted a specially-designed armoured turret operated by four men. Some of the design issues that killed the T36 project included an overly-complex fire-control system and poor access to the turret for maintenance. (*TACOM*)

(*Above*) Following in the footsteps of the 40mm GMC T36, the US army came up with the Multiple GMC T52 seen here. It was based on the chassis of a Medium Tank M4A2 and fitted with a new turret design armed with a 40mm Automatic Gun M1 and two large-calibre air-cooled machine guns. Testing of the T52 revealed a number of design issues that caused the project to be ended in October 1944. (*TACOM*)

(*Opposite above*) The 90mm GMC T53 as pictured came about because the US army was very impressed by the German employment of their 8.8cm gun in both the anti-aircraft and anti-tank roles and wanted to emulate it. The T53 consisted of the 90mm Gun M1 mounted on the modified chassis of a Medium Tank M4A4. Testing showed it to be unsuitable in either the anti-aircraft or anti-tank role and it was rejected. (*TACOM*)

(*Opposite below*) Lessons learned from the failure of the 90mm GMC T53 led the US army to build the 90mm GMC T53E1 seen here. The 90mm Gun M1 was moved to the centre of the M4A4 tank chassis on the T53E1 to better balance the gun when firing. Note the stored outriggers on the side of the vehicle's suspension system that would be deployed prior to firing when positioned on uneven terrain. As with the earlier 90mm GMC T53, the Tank Destroyer Board rejected the T53E1 as an anti-tank vehicle; it was considered a design dead-end and soon cancelled. (*TACOM*)

CHASSIS MED. TANK M4A1
WEIGHT 64700 LBS.
CRUISING SPEED 26 M.P.H.
CRUISING RADIUS 150 MILES
ARMAMENT 90 MM. A A GUN
AMMUNITION STOWAGE 68 RDS.
TRAVERSE 360°
MAXIMUM ELEVATION OF GUN 80°
MAXIMUM DEPRESSION OF GUN 11'

(*Opposite above*) Based on the chassis of a modified Light Tank M24 is this privately-owned and restored vehicle designated as the Twin 40mm GMC M19. The US army had originally envisioned fielding a companion vehicle also based on the Light Tank M24 chassis that was to carry additional 40mm ammunition for the M19. This was soon cancelled in favour of a two-wheeled ammunition trailer that could be towed behind the M19. (*Author's collection*)

(*Opposite below*) Shown at a US army testing centre is this vehicle based on the Light Tank M24 chassis and designated as the Multiple .50 calibre GMC T77. The vehicle was manned by a crew of four with a two-man gun crew in the powered turret and the driver and assistant driver in the front hull. There were 2,200 ready-rounds in the turret for immediate firing and another 3,400 stored in the hull. (*TACOM*)

(*Above*) Two self-propelled artillery pieces named the 'Bishop' by the British army are shown in this wartime image. The vehicle had a length of 18ft 2in, a width of 8ft 7.25in and a height of 9ft 3in. Maximum speed of the Bishop on level roads was 14mph and half that when travelling off-road. (*Tank Museum*)

(*Above*) Shown is a restored self-propelled artillery piece best known by its assigned wartime name of the 'Sexton'. It was the British and Commonwealth armies' counterpart to the US army 105mm HMC M7. It was armed with the QF 25-pounder (83mm) gun/howitzer. By the middle of 1944, the Canadian-developed and built Sexton had replaced all the American Lend-Lease-supplied M7s in British and Commonwealth army armoured divisions. (*Ian Wilcox*)

(*Opposite above*) The Canadian army saw a need for a tank-based self-propelled anti-aircraft vehicle and developed the vehicle seen here named the 'Skink'. It had a turret armed with four 20mm guns, this being the pilot turret design. However, Allied air superiority in the ETO meant that there was no real need for this type of specialized vehicle. (*Patton Museum*)

(*Opposite below*) The first version of the British Churchill tank series was armed with a QF 2-pounder (40mm) gun in its turret and a QF 3-inch Howitzer located in its front hull as seen here with this preserved example. The 2-pounder was the tank's main anti-tank armament but lacked an HE round to engage towed anti-tank guns. This was the reason for the fitting of the 3-inch howitzer, introduced into service in 1938, that could fire both an HE and a smoke round. (*Ian Wilcox*)

(*Above*) Pictured is a preserved British army cruiser tank labelled the 'Centaur IV'. This version of the series is armed with the QF 95mm Howitzer introduced into service in 1942. The Centaur was the direct predecessor of the British army cruiser tank named the 'Cromwell'. There were also two versions of the Cromwell series designated the VI and VIII armed with the QF 95mm Howitzer. (*Pierre-Olivier Buan*)

(*Opposite above*) There were also several versions of the Churchill infantry tank series seen here that were armed with the QF 95mm Howitzer. These included the Mark V, VII and XI models. Besides being able to fire both HE and smoke rounds, the QF 95mm Howitzer could also fire an approximately 14lb high-explosive anti-tank (HEAT) round when forced to engage enemy tanks. (*Tank Museum*)

(*Opposite below*) Encounters with German ground-attack aircraft during the Battle of France led to the production of anti-aircraft tanks. The example pictured here was labelled as the Tank, Light AA Mark II and was armed with four 7.92mm BESA medium machine guns in a one-man open-topped turret. The BESA was a licence-built model developed from the Czech ZB37 machine gun. (*Tank Museum*)

The machine-gun-armed turret from the Tank, Light AA Mark II was also fitted to the British army Humber 4 × 4 armoured car series. Vehicles so fitted were labelled as the Humber AA Mark I. The number constructed is unknown. The BESA machine gun fed from 225-round belts and was the standard armament of almost all British tanks and AFVs during the Second World War. (*Tank Museum*)

As the BESA 7.9mm Medium Machine Gun lacked both the range and knock-down power to reliably destroy German ground-attack aircraft, the British army therefore took the next step and mounted a single British licence-built copy of the Swedish-designed 40mm Bofors anti-aircraft gun on a tank chassis. The resulting vehicle shown here was designated as the Crusader II AA Mark I. (*Tank Museum*)

Another wartime tank-based anti-aircraft vehicle fielded by the British army is shown here. It was designated as the Crusader III AA Mark II and was fitted with a fully-enclosed turret armed with two British licence-built examples of the Swiss-designed 20mm Oerlikon gun. The guns were air-cooled and capable of a maximum rate of fire of 450 rounds per minute. (*Tank Museum*)

Pictured is the American-built Armoured Car T17E2 built to satisfy a British army requirement. It was the anti-aircraft version of the American-designed and built Armoured Car T17E1 named the 'Staghound' by the British army. The T17E2 was armed with two large .50 calibre air-cooled machine guns that were installed in a British-designed turret built in the United States. (*Patton Museum*)

On display at a Moscow military museum is this preserved Red Army KV-2 tank. It is armed with a 152mm gun/howitzer labelled as the L/20. The weapon was intended for the destruction of enemy bunkers, not enemy tanks. It fired an approximately 104lb HE round. Due to the size and weight of the round, the projectile and the cartridge case were loaded separately into the weapon's breech. (*Vladimir Yakubov*)

Here German soldiers are examining a knocked-out Red Army KV-2 tank that took penetrating hits to both its turret and 152mm gun/howitzer barrel. Almost all of the KV-2 tanks built were lost by the Red Army during the early months of the German invasion of the Soviet Union. The vehicle had a length of 22ft 10in, a width of 10ft 11in and a height of 10ft 8in. (*Patton Museum*)

On display is this preserved late-production SU-76M light self-propelled gun. The vehicle consisted of a 76.2mm divisional field gun mounted on the rear open-topped chassis of a lengthened and modified T-70 light tank. It would prove to be the second most-produced armoured fighting vehicle in the Red Army after the T-34 medium tank series. (*Bob Fleming*)

Upon the chassis of the SU-76 series the Red Army mounted a 37mm anti-aircraft gun in an open-topped armoured turret with 360 degrees of traverse. The combination was referred to as ZSU-37 and was authorized for production in 1944 with only a few hundred being built before the end of the war. The SU prefix stood for *Samokhodnaya Ustanovka*, Russian for self-propelled carriage. (*Vladimir Yakubov*)

Based on the chassis of the T-34 medium tank series is this preserved SU-122 Medium Self-Propelled Gun armed with the M-38 122mm howitzer. Its main armament could fire either an HE round or a HEAT round when engaging enemy tanks. The vehicle is 22ft 8in in length, has a width of 10ft 8in and a height of 8ft. *(Vladimir Yakubov)*

Like ancient beasts ascending from the primordial bog, SU-152 Heavy Self-Propelled Guns are shown exiting a river. The five-man vehicle was based on the chassis of the KV-1S Heavy Tank and armed with a 152mm gun/howitzer. The weapon was designated as the ML/20 and able to penetrate 110mm of armour at 2,187 yards. *(Bob Fleming)*

A German army NCO cradles a projectile from the destroyed Red Army SU-152 Heavy Self-Propelled Gun in the background. Due to the weight and size of the complete round, the projectile and cartridge case were loaded separately into the weapon's breech. Such a routine meant that the SU-152 had a rate of fire of only two rounds per minute. (*Bob Fleming*)

(*Opposite above*) In this wartime photograph we see a factory building the SU-152 Heavy Self-Propelled Gun for the Red Army. Note the large multi-slotted muzzle brake at the end of the barrel to reduce recoil. The vehicle was 29ft 4in in length, had a width of 10ft 8in and a height of 8ft. Armour thickness at the front of the vehicle was only 60mm. (*Bob Fleming*)

(*Above*) Pictured is a preserved ISU-152 Heavy Self-Propelled Gun built upon the chassis of the IS-2 Heavy Tank. It was the replacement for the SU-152 Heavy Self-Propelled Gun and retained the same main armament as its predecessor. In general configuration the two vehicles look very similar. However, the armoured casemate on the ISU-152 is higher and less steeply-sloped than that on the SU-152. (*Vladimir Yakubov*)

(*Opposite below*) On display at a Finnish army museum is this preserved ISU-152 Heavy Self-Propelled Gun. The typical role assigned to the vehicle was to support offensive breakthroughs by the Red Army and to neutralize enemy strongpoints and anti-tank defences with its large HE round. The ISU-152 was 29ft 7in in length with a width of 10ft and a height of 8ft 1in. (*Bob Fleming*)

In 1943 there was a shortage of the 152mm gun/howitzer to arm the ISU-152 Heavy Self-Propelled Gun. As there was a surplus at that time of the 122mm gun labelled as the A-19, it was decided to re-arm some of the intended ISU-152s with the 122mm gun. This resulted in the designation ISU-122, with two examples of the vehicle shown here taking part in a parade. (*Bob Fleming*)

With the late-war development of the IS-3 Heavy Tank the Red Army began looking at using the chassis to come up with a replacement for the ISU-152 Heavy Self-Propelled Gun. The single example of that train of thought that was not ordered into production is seen here and was labelled as the 'Object 704'. The front hull of the vehicle was protected by 120mm thick armour. (*Vladimir Yakubov*)

Chapter Four

Miscellaneous Vehicles

As the US army began thinking about the process of mechanization in the 1930s, it was clear that a vehicle would be needed to allow infantrymen to keep up with ever-faster tanks on the battlefield. This resulted in the December 1939 approval for the building of a pilot vehicle designated as the Half-Track Scout Car T14. Not willing to wait for the test data on the vehicle, the US army recommended in September 1940 that approval be given for the production of the T14 in three different versions.

The three proposed variants of the T14 included the Half-Track Car M2 with seating for ten men, which could also double as a reconnaissance or towing vehicle (prime mover) for artillery pieces or anti-tank guns. The second would be an 81mm mortar-carrying version of the Half-Track Car M2 labelled as the M4 and discussed in the previous chapter of this book. The final version of the T14 proposed was a lengthened version of the Half-Track Car M2 that could carry thirteen men and was designated as the Half-Track Personnel Carrier M3.

Production Begins

In October 1940, the US army gave approval for production of all three proposed models of the T14. The first production units of the Half-Track Car M2 rolled off the assembly line in May 1941. By the time production of the vehicle series ended in September 1943, a total of 11,415 units had been constructed. The role of the half-tracks in service with US army Armoured Divisions during the Second World War appears in this passage from a wartime field manual entitled the *Armored Infantry Battalion*:

> The half-track personnel carrier provides protection for the troops against small arms fire up to close-range. The armor also gives protection against bomb and shell fragments. Troops are transported as far forward as possible in each situation; terrain, cover, and the type of weapons available to the enemy governing the dismounting. The vehicular weapons are used to protect the attacking troops against air attack. Armor on the half-track does not protect crews against antitank weapons and direct hits by assault guns and light artillery.

In May 1943, a new machine-gun-armed ring mount designated as the M49 was authorized for fitting to all half-tracks coming off the production lines beginning in October 1943. With this addition the Half-Track Car M2 car became the M2A1 with a total of 1,643 units built in this configuration between October 1943 and March 1944. Under Lend-Lease the Free French army would be supplied with 176 units of the Half-Track Car M2 series.

Production of the Half-Track Personnel Carrier M3 also began in May 1941 with 12,391 units completed by September 1943. With the addition of the M49 machine-gun-armed ring mount, the Half-Track Personnel Carrier M3 became the M3A1. In this configuration a total of 2,882 units were built between October 1943 and June 1945. Both the M2 and M3 series half-tracks weighed approximately 20,000lb.

In addition to new-built M3A1s, the US army had 1,360 redundant units of the 75mm GMC M3 converted into the M3A1 configuration. The Free French army was provided with 245 units of the Half-Track Personnel Carrier M3 series under Lend-Lease.

There was a project begun by the US army in December 1942 aimed at coming up with a single half-track model that could replace both the Half-Track Car M2 and the Half-Track Personnel Carrier M3. It was to be based on the M3 and was eventually assigned the designation Half-Track Car M3A2. Production of the vehicle was to have begun in March 1944. However, by this time the user community was no longer interested in half-tracks but was in favour of full-tracked vehicles with their superior off-road performance.

Another Half-Track Builder Appears

The US army began to look for new manufacturers of its half-track in early 1942. The problem was that the existing builders – including White, the Autocar Company and the Diamond T Motor Company – lacked the industrial capacity to build as many as the US army anticipated needing for itself and for America's Lend-Lease commitments.

To meet the US army's requirements for more half-tracks, the International Harvester Company (IHC) was awarded a contract to build modified copies of the Half-Track Car M2 and Half-Track Personnel Carrier M3. Respectively the IHC copies would be designated as the Half-Track Car M9 and the Half-Track Personnel Carrier M5. Lessons learned by the US army from the earlier half-track designs resulted in the IHC-built half-tracks having stronger springs and axles fitted, pushing their weight up to approximately 21,000lb.

All the 3,433 production units of the Half-Track Car M9 built between March 1943 and December 1943 were fitted with the Ring Mount M49 and therefore designated as the Half-Track Car M9A1. There were 4,625 units of the Half-Track Personnel Carrier M5 built between December 1942 and September 1943. Those fitted with the Ring Mount M49 were labelled as the Half-Track Personnel Carrier M5A1 with 2,959 units constructed between October 1943 and March 1944.

The US army re-evaluated the number of half-tracks it believed would be required from a high of 188,404 units in February 1942 down to 87,302 units In October 1943. As the US army did not wish to mix IHC-built half-tracks with those built by the three original contractors in front-line units due to logistical issues, approximately half were assigned to Lend-Lease.

Of the 11,017 units of the IHC half-tracks assembled in the United States, the British army received 5,328 units under Lend-Lease. The Red Army received 420 IHC-built half-tracks and two Half-Track Personnel Carrier M3s through Lend-Lease. The Canadian army was supplied with twenty units of the IHC-built half-tracks via Lend-Lease. Those IHC half-tracks not allocated to Lend-Lease were retained in the United States for training purposes during the Second World War.

The US army had wanted to eventually replace both the Half-Track Car M9A1 and the Half-Track Personnel Carrier M5A1 with a single vehicle. It was to be designated as the Half-Track Car M5A2 but, like the Half-Track Car M3A2, it was never ordered into production.

Looking for Solutions

The biggest complaints from the user community were the half-track's poor off-road mobility and limited armour protection. To address these issues the US army had explored the possibility of fielding an improved up-armoured half-track. It was designated as the Half-Track Car T16 and consisted of the lengthened chassis of the Half-Track Car M2 with a redesigned suspension system. It also came with a raised armoured roof.

Testing of the T16 was unsatisfactory as the overhead armour arrangement reduced the vehicle's performance and the project was therefore cancelled. Also tested by the US army were the open-topped Half-Track Truck T17 and T19 intended as prime movers for artillery pieces in lieu of the M2 Half-Track Car. Neither met the expectations of the US army and never progressed past the pilot stage as unarmoured full-tracked prime movers had already taken over the role.

Full-Tracked Solutions

In early 1944, the US army began looking into employing a turretless version of the 76mm GMC M18 for two different roles. These would include acting as a prime mover replacement for the existing half-tracks being used to tow the 3-inch Gun Carriage M6. It was also considered as a possible replacement for the Light Armoured Car M8 and Armoured Utility Car M20 in tank destroyer units.

Testing of the turretless version of the 76mm GMC M18 pilots labelled as the Armoured Utility Vehicle T41 went very well. Production was soon authorized and 650 units would be converted from an existing inventory of early-production 76mm

GMC M18s into the Armoured Utility Vehicle M39. This was accomplished between October 1944 and March 1945.

The nine-man Armoured Utility Vehicle M39 began arriving in the ETO in very small numbers in early 1945 as the towed 3-inch Gun Carriage M6 had been pulled from service by this time. Those in theatre were employed in the reconnaissance role and as ad hoc armoured personnel carriers. Unfortunately, pictorial evidence of the approximately 35,000lb M39 performing these roles during the end stage of the war in the ETO is lacking.

In the autumn of 1944, the US army decided that it required a full-tracked multi-purpose vehicle that could perform a variety of roles including transportation of personnel. This led to the building of a pilot vehicle originally labelled as the Armoured Utility Vehicle T16 and later to become the M44. It had a crew of three and could carry twenty-four soldiers in its rear compartment, which included over-head armour protection. The end of the war in August 1945 led to the cancellation of the approximately 51,000lb M44 project.

As the US army defined an armoured personnel carrier as a vehicle intended only to carry an infantry squad, the M44 was too large for the role. This resulted in the US army setting a requirement in September 1945 for the development of a full-tracked twelve-man armoured personnel carrier. That vehicle was to have an armoured roof and was eventually designated as the Armoured Infantry Vehicle M75. Production of the approximately 41,500lb vehicle did not begin until 1952.

British/Commonwealth Army Armoured Personnel Carriers

In spite of the more than 5,000 units of the IHC-built M9 and M5 series half-tracks supplied to the British army under Lend-Lease, they were generally not employed by the British or Commonwealth armies as armoured personnel carriers, with excep-tions of course. Rather they were used in a number of other roles including as prime movers. For the armoured personnel carrier role the British and Commonwealth armies utilized the Universal Carrier described in the first chapter of this work.

The British and Commonwealth armies primarily saw the Universal Carrier as a battlefield taxi when assigned to infantry battalions. Their job was to transport machine-gun teams as close to the objective as possible before allowing them to dismount. The vehicles would then withdraw until called forward by the machine-gunners to remount and move on to the next objective. It was not unknown for the machine-gun-armed Universal Carriers to be employed in an offensive role. Universal Carriers were also employed at times to transport riflemen.

A Success Story

A much more successful armoured personnel carrier employed by the British and Canadian armies in North-West Europe was a series of improvised vehicles assigned the codename 'Kangaroo'. They were initially de-gunned American-built 105mm HMC M7 Priests reconfigured to carry as many as ten infantrymen besides the two-man crew.

The Kangaroos were an instant hit in August 1944 with the Canadian army because their mobility was the equal of the tanks they were supporting in battle. They also provided the infantrymen riding them into battle with a much higher level of armour protection than that offered by half-tracks or Universal Carriers, although they remained open-topped.

Because there was a much larger number of redundant Ram I and II Cruiser Tanks available to the British and Canadian armies than the 105mm HMC M7 Priest, it was quickly decided that the turretless chassis of these vehicles would become the Kangaroo platform of choice. In Italy, the British army converted both the 105mm HMC M7 Priest and turretless M4 series Medium Tanks into the Kangaroo con-figuration as they lacked access to any redundant Ram I and II Cruiser Tanks.

Full-Tracked Amphibious Vehicles

A vehicle class that was unique to the American military during the Second World War was the Landing Vehicle Tracked (LVT) series. The first was the LVT-1, of which 1,225 units were constructed between August 1941 and 1943. The vehicle weighed approximately 33,000lb.

The LVT-1 had originally been designed as an unarmed and unarmoured logistical supply vehicle. Nevertheless, the USMC decided to employ them as assault vehicles in November 1943. This was accomplished by applying improvised armour kits to them as well as fitting them with machine guns. Their success led to the USMC demanding the design and construction of superior LVTs.

The LVT-1 nicknamed the 'Alligator' was coming off the production line in the summer of 1942 at the same time as an improved model designated as the LVT-2. The LVT-2 was often referred to as an 'Amtrac' or 'tractor'. A total of 2,963 units would roll off the assembly line by 1945. As with the LVT-1, the LVT-2 was primarily intended as an unarmoured logistical supply vehicle but was also employed as an improvised assault vehicle along with the LVT-1 in November 1943.

Dedicated Amphibious Assault Vehicles

In response to the demand for factory-built armoured and armed LVTs, two additional vehicles were placed into development based on design modifications to the unarmoured LVT-2. The first in 1941 was the Landing Vehicle, Tracked, Armoured, Mark II or LVT(A)-2. Armed only with machine guns, 450 units of the open-topped vehicles were built. It first saw combat with the USMC during the assault on Cape Gloucester in December 1943.

The second vehicle was the Landing Vehicle, Tracked, Armoured, Mark I or LVT(A)-1. A total of 509 units of the vehicle were built between 1942 and 1944. The six-man vehicle was based on the LVT(A)-2 but with an enclosed rear cargo compartment upon its roof, a two-man light tank turret armed with a 37mm Gun M6 and a coaxial machine gun was fitted. In the rear of the vehicle's armoured roof were two armoured shield-protected machine-gun positions.

The LVT(A)-1 was also often referred to as a 'tank', an 'amtank' or 'amptank'. Its combat debut took place during the Battle of Kwajalein that lasted from January to February 1944. As combat experience quickly showed that the 37mm main gun on the LVT(A)-1 lacked the hitting power to destroy heavily-fortified Japanese bunkers, work was quickly begun on an up-gunned version of the vehicle designated as the LVT(A)-4, which appeared in service beginning in March 1944.

The LVT(A)-4 was armed with the 75mm Howitzer M3 in an open-topped armoured turret whose design was borrowed from the M8 HMC. A total of 1,307 units of the approximately 40,000lb vehicle rolled off the assembly line between 1944 and 1945. The six-man LVT(A)-4 proved too lightly armoured to survive on the battlefield as a tank and was soon pushed into using its main armament in the indirect fire role.

In April 1945, the LVT(A)-4 turret was provided with a powered traverse system. Reflecting this upgrade to the vehicle's design, it was redesignated as the LVT(A)-5.

Correcting a Design Issue

The biggest design fault with the LVT-1 and the LVT-2 series was their lack of a rear ramp that forced cargo to be loaded or removed by hand over the sides of the vehicles or with the aid of an overhead crane. For personnel it forced all to embark or disembark from the vehicle by climbing over the sides of its hull, which could be a serious problem when under enemy fire.

The access problem regarding cargo and personnel with the LVT-2 was solved with a redesigned version that came with a rear ramp and was designated the LVT-4. It first saw use in the summer of 1944 during the invasion of Saipan, part of the Marianas Island chain. A total of 8,348 units of the vehicle were constructed between 1943 and 1945. The US navy went on to transfer 6,083 units of the LVT-4 to the US army. Approximately 500 units of the LVT-4 went to the British army under Lend-Lease who labelled it the 'LVT Buffalo' and armed them with a 20mm gun plus machine guns.

Another LVT with a rear-loading ramp was designated as the Landing Vehicle, Tracked, Mark III or LVT-3 and began rolling off the production line in 1944. The designer and builder named it the 'Bushmaster'. By the time production of the LVT-3 concluded in 1945, a total of 2,962 units had been completed. The vehicle did not enter into combat until the last year of the war. As the newest and most advanced design of all the wartime LVTs, it was the only vehicle retained post-war by the US navy for use by the USMC.

Red Army Flame-Thrower Tanks

The Red Army began development of a flame-thrower version of its T-26 Light Tank series in 1932. In Red Army service flame-thrower tanks were originally referred to as 'Chemical Tanks' and later as Flame-thrower Tanks (OT: *Ognemetniy* Tank). The original version was based on the twin-turreted version of the T-26 before switching to what became the standard single-turreted model in 1935. That model of the vehicle was designated as the KhT-26.

By 1939 the Red Army came to the conclusion that its flame-thrower tanks needed an onboard main gun to defend themselves from a host of battlefield threats. What appeared in service the following year was a T-26 that retained its turret-mounted 45mm main gun and had its flame-thrower moved to the front of the vehicle's hull. There were two versions labeled the KhT-130 and KhT-133.

The usefulness of the T-26-based flame-thrower tanks was proven in fighting the Japanese army between 1938 and 1939 and in combat with the Finnish army between 1939 and 1940. With the loss of the bulk of its inventory of T-26 tanks in the summer of 1941 with the German invasion, the Red Army developed a flame-thrower kit in 1942 that could be fitted in the bow machine-gun position of the T-34 Medium Tank series. Vehicles so fitted were redesignated as the OT-34.

The Red Army also modified a version of their KV-1 Heavy Tank series to be fitted with a hull-mounted flame-thrower. As there was insufficient room in the turret of the vehicle for the flame gun and storage tanks, the standard 76.2mm main gun was replaced by a smaller 45mm main gun. To prevent early identification of the vehicle labelled as the KV-8, the smaller 45mm main gun normally had a metal tube fitted over it to replicate the appearance of the original 76.2mm main gun. There was also a KV-8S version based on a KV-1S.

American Military Flame-Thrower Tanks

Prior to America's entry into the Second World War in December 1941, the US army had begun exploring the concept of flame-thrower tanks. Experiments were conducted with de-gunned examples of first the Medium Tank M2 and then the Medium Tank M3. The first effective flame-thrower tank consisted of a British-designed flame gun named the Ronson mounted in the front hull of twenty-four USMC M3A1 Light Tanks. The resulting vehicle was nicknamed the 'Satan'.

Eventually an American-designed and built flame-thrower was fitted into the turret of the Light Tank M5A1 and the vehicle labelled as the Mechanized Flame-thrower E7-7. Only four examples were built as both the US army and USMC decided that the M4 Medium Tank was a better choice as a flame-thrower platform due to its thicker armour protection. This allowed it to engage targets at closer ranges without fear of early destruction. This was an issue that had affected both the light tank-based flame-thrower tanks as well as LVTs armed with flame-throwers.

Medium Tank-Based Flame-Throwers

Initially the US army tested the concept of front hull-mounted flame-thrower units on M4 Medium Tanks. However, the short range of the existing flame-thrower units and their low fuel capacity limited their usefulness. It was eventually decided that turret-mounted flame guns on de-gunned M4 Medium Tanks was the best option. This resulted in a vehicle designated as the POA-CWS-H1.

In October 1944, the US army transferred the first eight examples of the POA-CWS-H1 to the USMC, which would employ them during the battle for Iwo Jima in early 1945. The US army would employ fifty-four units of the POA-CWS-H1 during the fighting on the island of Okinawa from April 1945 to June 1945 with great effect.

As both the US army and USMC saw a need for their new M4 Medium Tank-based flame-thrower tanks to retain their main armament for self-protection, the follow-on to the POA-CWS-H1 was the POA-CWS-H5. A total of seventy units of the POA-CWS-H5 were eventually constructed but they arrived too late to see combat in the PTO.

The US army had also been working on incorporating a next-generation flame-thrower into the turrets of M4 series Medium Tanks. The Mechanized Flame-thrower M5-4 was the first and entered into production in late 1944 with 151 units built before production was halted. The follow-on Mechanized Flame-throwers based on the M4 Medium Tank series, which included the E13-13, E19-19 and T33, never progressed past the pilot stage before production was halted.

Ten of the new flame-thrower units were also mounted in the turrets of the LVT(A)-1. With the new flame-thrower fitted, they became the Mechanized Flame-thrower E14-7R2.

Universal Carrier-Based Flame-Throwers

Prior to the start of the Second World War neither the British army nor any of the Commonwealth armies had envisioned a requirement for flame-thrower vehicles. However, with the fall of France in the summer of 1940, the British army soon reconsidered and began experimenting with flame-thrower units mounted on the Universal Carrier. This eventually led to production orders for flame-thrower vehicles based on the Universal Carrier designated as the Wasp Mark I and the Wasp Mark II.

A total of 1,000 units of the Wasp Mark I were built between September 1942 and November 1943 for the British army, with production then being switched to the redesigned and improved Wasp Mark II, which was built between August 1943 and June 1944. The Canadian army did not think much of the Wasp Mark I but was much more impressed by its successor and ordered 500 flame-thrower kits designed for the Wasp II for fitting to a portion of its inventory of Universal Carriers. Vehicles so equipped were designated as the Mark IIC by the Canadian army.

British and Commonwealth Tank-Based Flame-Throwers

All realized that the open-topped and lightly-armoured Universal Carrier was not the optimum platform for a flame-thrower. This would lead to the development and fielding of tank-based flame-thrower vehicles by both the British and various Commonwealth armies. The first to see combat during the unsuccessful Dieppe Raid on 19 August 1942 were three Canadian army vehicles labelled as the 'Churchill Mark I Oke'. The fuel storage containers for the flame guns on the vehicles were located in an armoured compartment attached to the vehicle's rear hull.

Continued work on such systems resulted in the production of another flame-thrower version of the Churchill tank named the 'Crocodile'. Rather than have its fuel storage tanks attached to the rear hull of the vehicle, a two-wheeled towed armoured trailer was developed that fed its fuel to the flame gun located in the front hull of the Crocodile and could be jettisoned if needed. Production of the vehicle began late in 1944 and continued until the end of the war with 800 units completed. They saw action only in the ETO.

The Australian army developed a flame-thrower tank in 1944 referred to as the 'Matilda Frog'. It was replaced by an improved version in 1945 referred to as the 'Matilda Murray'. Both were based on the British-supplied Matilda II Infantry Tank. The Canadian army modified some of its Ram II Medium Tanks that had been converted into Kangaroos with a flame-thrower unit and renamed vehicles so fitted as the 'Badger'.

Mine-Clearance Vehicles

A number of avenues were explored by the wartime Allies to deal with enemy minefields; more so by the Western Allied armies rather than the Red Army. These included various types of mine-exploder systems, which included flail systems, pressure rollers and discs favoured by the Red Army and wedge-shaped mine excavators as well as concussion-type mine-exploders.

The first Allied mine-exploder flail device was British-designed and built and assigned the name 'Scorpion'. It was eventually fitted in different versions to a number of British-built and American Lend-Lease-supplied tanks. An improved follow-on British-designed and built version was named the 'Crab' with there being both a Mark I and Mark II model. The US army developed and fielded its own mine-exploder flail device designated as the T3 that was a failure in service.

The biggest problem with using pressure rollers and discs to detonate mines was the size and weight required to perform the task with any degree of success. This meant that they were extremely difficult to move from one location to another and therefore had to be constantly assembled and disassembled, a very time-consuming process. They also proved very vulnerable to relatively large explosive charges and delayed-action mine fuses.

Dealing with Enemy Fortifications

To deal with enemy defensive positions and obstacles, the US army decided on using large rockets as they packed enough explosive power to hopefully deal with any potential fortifications encountered on the battlefield. The first rocket-launcher units were mounted on the turret roofs of tanks. This was followed by rocket-launchers fitted inside tank turrets. The latter would not be placed into production.

The British army solution was to take redundant Churchill tanks and re-arm them with a direct-fire turret-mounted 290mm spigot mortar nicknamed the 'Petard'. They fired a 40lb high-explosive demolition projectile referred to as the 'Flying Dustbin' up to a range of 240ft. These vehicles were designated as the Churchill Armoured Vehicle, Royal Engineers (AVRE), and a total of 754 units were eventually built.

One of the simplest and most successful engineering devices fielded by the US army was an add-on bulldozer kit for the M4 Medium Tank series beginning in late 1943. Within armoured units the bulldozer-equipped tanks were employed to reduce both natural and man-made obstacles and prepare defensive positions if the need arose. The only disadvantage with the bulldozer kits was their weight that sometimes caused failure of the suspension systems of the tanks thus fitted.

This picture shows the interior layout of the pilot Half-Track Car T14, which later became the Half-Track Car M2. There was seating for ten men in the vehicle, with three seats on either side of the rear hull compartment facing inwards. The other four seats were divided between three in the driving compartment and one facing rearward between the vehicle's storage compartments. (TACOM)

An official photograph of the Half-Track Car M2 fitted with canvas foul-weather gear. The vehicle was protected by bolted-together face-hardened armour 6.4mm thick on all surfaces except for the 12.7mm thick armoured windshield, which could be raised or lowered depending on battlefield conditions. The vehicle's armour was intended to stop 7.92mm AP rounds at 200 yards. (*TACOM*)

Pictured at a re-enactment event is a restored Half-Track Car M2. The vehicle is 19ft 5in long, has a width of 6ft 4in and a height of 7ft 4in. Power comes from a six-cylinder gasoline-powered engine that provides the M2 with a maximum speed on level roads of 45mph and an approximate cruising range on roads of 200 miles. (*Bob Fleming*)

On display at a historical military vehicle rally is this restored Half-Track Car M2. The vehicle's front wheels were equipped with leaf springs. The VVSS system at the rear of the vehicle rode on two 12in-wide rubber tracks that had been vulcanized over steel cabling. The M2 could climb a vertical wall 12in high and had a fording depth of 32in. *(Pierre-Olivier Buan)*

When the Half-Track Car M2 was fitted with the machine-gun-armed Ring Mount M49 it was designated as the Half-Track Car M2A1. The restored M2A1 shown here is taking part in a historical military vehicle rally. On the lower portion of the vehicle's rear hull is a storage rack for carrying anti-tank mines, which is duplicated on the other side of the M2A1. *(Author's collection)*

Due to the skate rail that ran around the interior of the Half-Track Car M2A1, the vehicle was not designed with a rear door. On the rear of the M2A1 vehicle's hull pictured here we can see the tripod for the onboard large-calibre air-cooled machine gun. Also visible is the pintle-mounted onboard small-calibre air-cooled machine gun. (*TACOM*)

In this picture of a Half-Track Car M2A1 that has run over a mine in the ETO we see open one of the two large storage compartments located on either side of the vehicle's hull. They were originally intended for ammunition storage when the vehicle was being employed as a prime mover. Note the large wooden crate strapped to the rear of the vehicle's superstructure for additional storage. (*Patton Museum*)

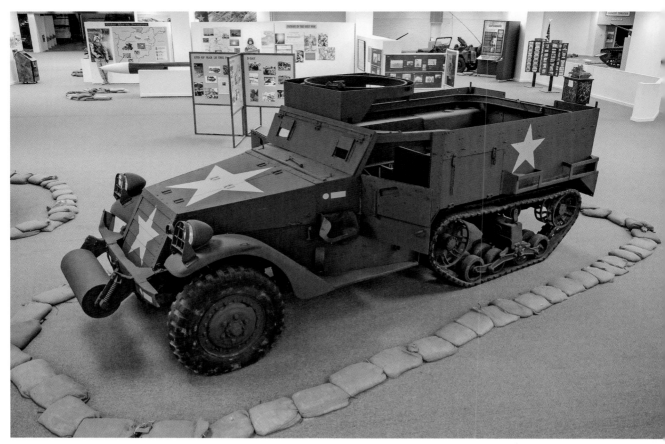

On display at a US army museum is this preserved Half-Track Car M2A1. Note the internal skate rail that allowed the pintle-mounted onboard machine guns to be moved around the interior of the M2 and the M2A1. At the right rear of the vehicle can be seen one of the two onboard fuel tanks, which held a total of 60 gallons of fuel. *(Paul Hannah)*

Coming off the production line at the same time as the Half-Track Car M2 was the Half-Track Personnel Carrier M3 shown here during a training exercise in the United States. Despite its designation as a personnel carrier M3, the vehicle served in a variety of roles including command and control as might be indicated by the antennas seen on the vehicle pictured. *(Patton Museum)*

The Half-Track Personnel Carrier M3 was 10in longer than the Half-Track Car M2. It also lacked the two storage compartments of its shorter counterpart. This meant that the M3 had seating for thirteen soldiers as seen here rather than the ten of the M2. Note the gun mount just behind the driver's compartment and the lack of an interior skate rail. (TACOM)

When the Half-Track Personnel Carrier M3 was fitted with the Ring Mount M49 armed with a large-calibre machine gun, it was redesignated as the Half-Track Personnel Carrier M3A1. The M49 Ring Mount can be clearly seen on the M3A1 pictured taking part in a historical military rally at the former Patton Museum of Cavalry and Armor. (Chun-lun Hsu)

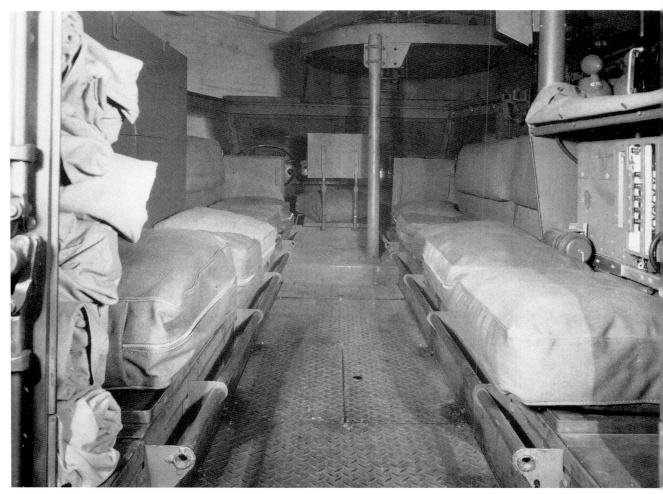

(*Above*) Reflecting their primary role as an infantry transport vehicle, the Half-Track Personnel Carrier M3 and M3A1 were designed with a rear hull armoured door. This photograph was taken through the open rear armoured door of an M3A1 looking forward. Visible is the steel post that supports the rear of the M49 Ring Mount. To the right of the picture behind the seats a radio is visible. (*TACOM*)

(*Opposite above*) This restored Half-Track Personnel Carrier M3A1 can be identified as a later-production example as it is fitted with a 10,000lb capacity winch instead of the front-mounted roller seen on earlier-production units. A power take-off from the vehicle's transmission provided the power to the winch. The rear propeller shaft powered the vehicle's rear axle and the two drive sprockets. (*Christophe Vallier*)

(*Opposite below*) Shown taking part in a historical military vehicle rally is this restored Half-Track Personnel Carrier M3A1. The rifle squad that rode the M3 and M3A1 into combat consisted of twelve men, which included the squad leader, the assistant squad leader and nine infantrymen. The vehicle's driver always remained with his vehicle and was typically armed with a sub-machine gun. (*Bob Fleming*)

Being run is a restored Half-Track Personnel Carrier M3A1 at a tank museum annual event known as 'Tankfest'. When a US army infantry squad disembarked from its M3 or M3A1, the large-calibre machine gun seen on this vehicle (in this case a replica) was typically left on the vehicle due to its weight and size. Instead, the rifle squad would often take into action a more portable small-calibre machine gun. (*Christophe Vallier*)

A knocked-out Half-Track Personnel Carrier M3A1 in the ETO. In spite of the many complaints about the thin armour, lack of overhead armour protection and poor off-road mobility for the entire M2 and M3 series, half-tracks were widely employed by the US army during the Second World War. They were what American industry could design and build cheaply and in large numbers at the time. (*Christophe Vallier*)

To supplement the production of the M2 and M3 series half-tracks and provide enough half-tracks for its own use as well as Lend-Lease, the US army awarded contracts to the International Harvester Corporation (IHC) to build modified versions of the existing M2 and M3 series half-tracks. Pictured is the IHC counterpart to the Half-Track Personnel Carrier M3 designated as the Half-Track Personnel Carrier M5. *(TACOM)*

Pictured is a restored Half-Track Personnel Carrier M5 built by the International Harvester Corporation (IHC). Rather than being built from faced-armoured plates bolted together as was the Half-Track Personnel Carrier M3, the M5 was constructed of homogenous armour plates welded together. An external difference between the M3 and M5 is their respective front fender designs. *(Chun-lun Hsu)*

When the Half-Track Personnel Carrier M5 built by the International Harvester Corporation was fitted at the factory with the M49 Ring Mount, it was redesignated as the M5A1. Due to their construction method the IHC-built half-tracks had rounded rear corners as seen in this photograph instead of the 90 degree-angled butt joints of the M2 and M3 series of half-tracks. *(TACOM)*

The International Harvester Corporation-built counterpart of the Half-Track Car M2A1 was the Half-Track Car M9A1 seen here fitted with the Ring Mount M49. Unlike the M2A1, the M9A1 was the same length as the Half-Track Personnel Carrier M5/M5A1 and was fitted with a rear hull door. It did not have the two hull side storage compartments of the M2 or M2A1. *(TACOM)*

The US army was not unaware that the thin armour protection of its entire half-track inventory and lack of overhead protection would pose problems for the user community in combat. Early on the US army came up with a much-modified Half-Track Car M2 seen here and designated as the T16. It had a more robust suspension system with wider tracks plus overhead armour protection but failed to live up to the US army's expectations. (*TACOM*)

As a replacement for the Half-Track Car M2/M2A1 in the prime mover role the US army evaluated a number of possible half-track candidate vehicles that it referred to as 'half-track trucks'. Pictured is the Half-Track Truck T17 version. By the time the pilots like the T17 were being tested, the US army was only interested in full-track prime movers and all work on the half-track trucks soon ended. (*TACOM*)

Shown is a restored example of an Armoured Utility Vehicle M39. The vehicle had a length of 17ft 4in, a width of 9ft 0.5in and a height of 6ft 7in. Armament was typically a single large-calibre machine gun. The armour on the front and sides of the hull was 12.5mm thick. On level road the M39 could reach a maximum speed of 50mph. (TACOM)

The intended replacement for the Armoured Utility Vehicle M39 was the Armoured Utility Vehicle M44 shown here. It had a crew of twenty-seven men which included a driver, bow gunner, vehicle commander and twenty-four infantrymen. The thickest armour on the M44 was only 16mm. Vehicle length was 21ft 4in with a width of 9ft 11in and a height of 8ft 4in. (TACOM)

Conceived in the same month that the Second World War came to an end was the Armoured Utility Vehicle T18 seen here as a wooden mock-up. It was designed to carry only twelve men, which would comprise a driver, vehicle commander and ten infantrymen. When finally approved for production, a modified version of the T18 labelled as the T18E1 became the Armoured Infantry Vehicle M75. (*TACOM*)

On display in front of a Canadian army museum is this preserved Universal Carrier. The first production order for the vehicle was awarded in April 1939. The actual origins of the Universal Carrier can be traced back to 1927 when Carden-Loyd (acquired by Vickers-Armstrong the following year) began building for the British army a small two-man machine-gun carrier labelled the Mark IV. (*Paul Hannah*)

The Universal Carrier seen here on museum display is often confused with the Carrier, Bren, which is better known as the 'Bren Gun Carrier'. However, the latter predates the former with production beginning in 1937. Besides being armed with the .303 (7.7mm) Bren machine gun seen here mounted on the vehicle pictured, some were also armed with the .55 Boys Anti-tank Rifle.
(Alan Wilcox)

The restored Universal Carrier pictured here is armed with two machine guns: an air-cooled .303 (7.7mm) Bren machine gun and a .303 Vickers water-cooled machine gun. The British-designed and built Vickers machine gun had entered service with the British army in 1912. The Bren machine gun was a licence-built version of a Czech-designed machine gun and entered British army service in 1937. *(Christophe Vallier)*

Belonging to a private collector is this restored Canadian army open-topped armoured personnel carrier designated as the C15TA Armoured Truck. It was designed and built by General Motors of Canada and between 1944 and 1945 a total of 3,961 units of the approximately 10,000lb vehicle were built. It was employed by both the Canadian and British armies in the ETO. (Author's collection)

Pictured is a restored Ram Kangaroo armoured personnel carrier. The version pictured is based on the redundant turretless chassis of the Canadian-designed and built Ram I Cruiser tank. According to British tank historian David Fletcher they were also referred to as 'sawn-off Rams'. The term Kangaroo was also applied to other redundant full-tracked vehicles converted into improvised armoured personnel carriers. (Tank Museum)

(*Opposite above*) In this wartime photograph we see a Ram Kangaroo armoured personnel carrier in the ETO. Each Ram Kangaroo could carry eight infantrymen besides the driver and the front hull machine-gunner. As the vehicle rode on the American-designed Medium Tank M3 suspension system it had no problem operating off-road when supporting most Allied tanks except for the Churchill Infantry Tank series. (*Tank Museum*)

(*Opposite below*) Soviet industry concentrated its resources during the Second World War on the building of as many tanks and self-propelled guns as possible. There was no spare industrial capacity for the construction of suitable armoured personnel carriers. The Red Army therefore added hand-holds to its tanks so that its infantrymen could ride into battle on them. This practice is seen here during a historical military vehicle rally. (*Christophe Vallier*)

(*Above*) The US Marine Corps anticipated problems in trying to cross the coral reefs surrounding Tarawa Atoll in November 1943 with the existing US navy flat-bottomed landing craft. They therefore decided to armour and arm a number of the US navy's full-tracked amphibious logistical vehicles referred to as the Landing Vehicle, Tracked, Mark I or LVT-1. Here we see one of those improvised LVT-1 assault vehicles knocked out during the capture of the Tarawa Atoll. (*Patton Museum*)

On display at a US Marine Corps museum is the sole surviving example of a US navy Landing Vehicle, Tracked, Mark I or LVT-1. The vehicle had never been intended for a combat role and had been built of mild steel. Propulsion in the water for the LVT-1 was achieved by the cleats (grousers) visible on the vehicle's tracks. Maximum water speed was 7mph and on land 18mph. (*Paul Hannah*)

Both the US navy and USMC were unhappy with the short mechanical lifespan of the Landing Vehicle, Tracked, Mark I or LVT-1 among other complaints. In response American industry designed an improved, larger and heavier version seen here classified as the Landing Vehicle, Tracked, Mark II or LVT-2. Like the LVT-1, the LVT-2 was unarmoured but on occasion was armoured and armed in the field. (*Patton Museum*)

To complement the Landing Vehicle, Tracked, Mark II or LVT-2 American industry designed and built an armoured version of the vehicle seen here that was labelled as the Landing Vehicle, Tracked, Armoured, Mark II or LVT(A)-2. Reflecting the extra weight of the armour added to the vehicle it was slower in the water and on land than the non-armoured LVT-2. *(Patton Museum)*

In this wartime photograph we see a Landing Vehicle, Tracked, Armoured, Mark I or LVT(A)-1. The vehicle had a length of 26ft 1in, a width of 10ft 8in and a height of 10ft 1in. The thickest armour on the vehicle was the turret gun shield at 51mm. The thickest portion of the LVTA-1 hull was the armoured cab at 13mm. There was onboard authorized storage for 104 rounds for the M6 37mm Gun. *(Patton Museum)*

(Above) The 37mm gun-armed turret seen here that was fitted to the Landing Vehicle, Tracked, Armoured, Mark I LVT(A)-1 was derived from that designed for the Light Tank M3 series. Behind the power-operated turret can be seen one of the two shield-protected small-calibre machine-gun positions that formed the normal armament of the LVT(A)-1. (Patton Museum)

(Opposite above) Belonging to the US army museum system is this restored Landing Vehicle, Tracked, Armoured, Mark I or LVT(A)-1. On land the vehicle's gasoline-powered radial engine could propel the vehicle at a top speed of 25mph on level ground. The maximum water speed of the LVT(A)1 was 6.5mph. The vehicle's powertrain, like the turret, came from the Light Tank M3 series. (Henry Penn)

(Opposite below) In a desire to add more firepower to the Landing Vehicle, Tracked, Armoured, Mark I or LVT(A)-1 there appeared the Landing Vehicle, Tracked, Armoured, Mark IV or LVT(A)-4 shown here. Gone was the 37mm gun-armed turret from the LVT(A)-1, replaced by the 75mm howitzer-armed turret from the 75mm HMC M8. The open-topped turret on the LVT(A)-4 was manually-operated. (Patton Museum)

The Landing Vehicle, Tracked, Armoured, Mark IV or LVT(A)-4s pictured here are early-production units as indicated by the large-calibre machine guns fitted to the turret. Combat showed that whoever operated the weapon was extremely vulnerable. In order to reduce the casualty rate among the machine-gunners there was an armoured parapet added to the front and sides of the turret roof as seen in this picture. *(Patton Museum)*

Eventually it was decided to remove the unprotected large-calibre machine gun from the turret of the Landing Vehicle, Tracked, Armoured, Mark IV or LVT(A)-4. In its place appeared two shield-protected small-calibre machine guns positioned as seen on the roof of the preserved LVT(A)-4 pictured here minus the actual machine guns. *(Christophe Vallier)*

The LVT-4 seen here was a redesigned LVT-2 equipped with a rear-loading ramp. This was achieved by moving the engine in the LVT-2 located in the rear of the vehicle's hull to a position behind the LVT-4 operator's cab. The LVT-4 could transport up to thirty infantrymen or small wheeled vehicles or small artillery pieces. *(Patton Museum)*

Unlike the earlier LVTs such as the LVT-1 and LVT-2 that had been strictly seen as unarmoured logistical transport vehicles with no expectancy of being employed in combat, the LVT-4 was designed from the beginning to accept factory-designed and built armouring kits that could be fitted in the field if the need arose. On the LVT-4 pictured in this wartime image we see the addition of two shield-protected small-calibre machine-gun positions minus their machine guns. *(Real War Photos)*

In general configuration the Landing Vehicle, Tracked, Mark III (LVT-3) resembled the LVT-4. However, they differed somewhat as the cab of the LVT-3 was located further forward on the hull than on the LVT-4. Pictured is a preserved example of an LVT-3. The vehicle had been designed with the provision to accept both factory-built armour kits and weapons if required. *(Christophe Vallier)*

Pictured is a group of unarmoured Landing Vehicle, Tracked, Mark IIIs (LVT-3s) at sea. The vehicle did not show up in the Pacific Theatre of Operation (PTO) until the invasion of Japanese-defended of Okinawa, which began in April 1945 and lasted until June 1945. The LVT-3 was 24ft 6in in length, 11ft 2in wide and 9ft 11in in height. *(Patton Museum)*

On display is this preserved LVT-3C. This was a post-war modified version of the wartime LVT-3 with an aluminium cover over its cargo compartment and an armoured cab fitted with a one-man machine-gun-armed turret. A total of 1,200 units of the LVT-3 were converted into the LVT-3C configuration with some seeing service during the Korean War. (*Patton Museum*)

The most numerous of the many specialized variants of the Red Army's large pre-war inventory of T-26 light tanks were various versions of flame-thrower tanks. The model pictured here was designated as the KhT-26 or XT-26. It was based on the chassis of the T-26 Model 1931 tank. The two original small one-man turrets were replaced with a single one-man turret armed with a flame gun. (*Bob Fleming*)

Based on the Red Army T-26 Model 1933 light tank was a second-generation flame-thrower tank seen here at a Russian museum and designated as the KhT-130. Rather than employing a specialized turret as seen on the KhT-26, the KhT-130 retained the tank's original turret and replaced the onboard 45mm main gun with a flame gun. *(Vladimir Yakubov)*

A German army intelligence photograph of a captured flame-thrower version of the KV-1 heavy tank referred to as the KV-8. To make room for the flame-thrower gun, the original 76.2mm main gun was replaced by a smaller 45mm main gun to provide the vehicle with a limited ability to defend itself against enemy vehicles. *(Patton Museum)*

The US army's first attempt at developing a suitable flame-thrower tank prior to America's official entry into the Second World War involved a modified Medium Tank M2. As the US army was quickly moving on to newer generations of medium tanks, the second flame-thrower pilot tank seen here was based on the Medium Tank M3 and was armed with a turret-mounted E3 flame gun. *(Patton Museum)*

Jungle-fighting in the PTO in late 1942 and early 1943 led both the US army units and USMC to conclude that an armour-protected flame-thrower would be more survivable than man-portable flame-throwers. Pictured is an early improvised example of an M3A1 Light Tank with a flame-thrower gun fitted in place of its front hull-mounted machine gun. *(Patton Museum)*

(*Above*) It was soon concluded by both the US army and the USMC that the armour protection on its light tanks was too thin and the range of the flame-thrower guns too short to make them reasonably survivable on the battlefield. This pushed the development of flame-thrower guns mounted in the bow gunner's position of better-protected M4 series medium tanks as seen here. (*Patton Museum*)

(*Opposite above*) Late in 1944, the US army and USMC began pressing for flame-thrower guns to be mounted in the turrets of M4 series medium tanks rather than in the bow gunner's position. This led to the building of a number of in-theatre examples labelled as the POA-CWS-H1. One is seen here in action with the USMC on the island of Iwo Jima in early 1945. (*Patton Museum*)

(*Opposite below*) Those using the POA-CWS-H1s decided that flame-thrower tanks needed to retain their 75mm main guns for self-protection and to remain useful when their flame-gun fuel was exhausted. This would lead to the development of an in-theatre vehicle seen here designated as the POA-CWS-H5. However, they arrived too late to see combat. (*Patton Museum*)

(*Opposite above*) In a separate line of development the US army was officially working on its own M4 series medium tank-based flame-thrower tanks beginning in early 1944. Pictured is the pilot vehicle for that work designated as the E13-13 Mechanized Flame-Thrower. The 75mm main gun was replaced on the vehicle by a new flame gun. To disguise the vehicle's purpose, it was fitted with a fake barrel. (*Richard Hunnicutt*)

(*Opposite below*) The US army eventually decided to stop work on the E13-13 Mechanized Flame-Thrower. They then moved on, beginning in May 1945, to a next-generation example seen here. It was designated as the Flame-Thrower Tank T33 and a specially-designed turret armed with the brand-new flame-thrower gun E20-20 and the 75mm M6 Gun from the Light Tank M24. Only three pilots were built before the vehicle project was cancelled. (*Patton Museum*)

(*Above*) The best-known British army flame-thrower tank was the 'Churchill Crocodile', a preserved example of which is seen here. The vehicle's flame-thrower gun was mounted in the front hull in place of the bow machine gun. Visible in this photograph is the heavy steel counterweight that was fitted over the muzzle end of the flame gun to better balance the weapon for the operator. (*Pierre-Olivier Buan*)

(*Opposite above*) Rather than having the highly volatile fuel for the flame-thrower gun mounted in the Churchill Crocodile stored within it, the fuel was stored in a specially-designed two-wheeled armoured trailer towed behind the vehicle as shown in this picture of a preserved example. The fuel was run from the trailer by hose under the vehicle's hull to the flame-gunner's compartment. (*Pierre-Olivier Buan*)

(*Opposite below*) To deal with the threat of mines in North Africa, the British army developed and fielded a device referred to as the 'Scorpion Mine Exploder'. It consisted of a powered rotating drum with attached chains that flailed the ground in front of whatever tank it was attached to in the hope of detonating the mines in its path. In this picture we see the original model attached to the front of a Matilda II Infantry Tank. (*Tank Museum*)

(*Above*) Pictured is the US army counterpart of the British army Scorpion Mine Exploder designated as the Mine Exploder T3. A total of forty-one units were built but they proved a failure in the field and all were later withdrawn from service. Two problems with the T3 were its weight and width, which greatly limited its off-road mobility. (*TACOM*)

The Scorpion Mine Exploder did not prove all that reliable in service with the British army in North Africa. This resulted in continued developmental work on trying to improve the concept. What eventually evolved was the 'Crab Mine Exploder' seen here, mounted on a preserved Canadian-built Grizzly tank. The Crab was a much more successful design and served with both the British and US army in the ETO. *(Paul Hannah)*

Both the British and US army experimented with roller-type mine-exploders. The British army concluded that they were not a workable solution and none were ever ordered into production. The US army, on the other hand, pursued the concept and eventually ordered production of a small number. Pictured here mounted on a M4 series medium tank is the T1E3 Mine Exploder. *(Patton Museum)*

To increase the traction of its roller-type mine-exploders on rough ground the US army began adding serrated edges to the mine roller discs as seen in this picture. The device pictured was designated as the T14 Mine Exploder. A later model with two extra discs was labelled as the T16. Only five units of the T14/T16 were built during the latter half of 1945 and did not see service in combat. *(TACOM)*

Rather than having a separate roller-type mine-exploder that would be pushed into action by a tank, somebody had the bright idea of turning an M4 series medium tank into a self-propelled mine roller exploder. The much-modified pilot vehicle seen here was labelled as the T10 Mine Exploder. US army testing of the pilot was not a success and it was never ordered into production. *(TACOM)*

One method for breaching enemy minefields tested by the US army involved firing explosive projectiles onto an enemy minefield with spigot mortars and hoping the resulting explosions would detonate enough mines to allow passage by friendly forces. Pictured is the T12 Mine Exploder with the launching rails for 115lb HE mortar rounds, which are not fitted in this image. (TACOM)

The unsuccessful Dieppe Raid in France on 19 August 1942 led to the development of a number of specialized engineering tank-based vehicles by the British army. One of them was intended to destroy enemy concrete beach fortifications and was designated as the Armoured Vehicle, Royal Engineers (AVRE). It consisted of a Churchill Infantry Tank armed with a turret-mounted 205mm spigot mortar as seen here. (Pierre-Olivier Buan)

The US army's response to the unsuccessful Dieppe Raid was to begin exploring the concept of using tank-based rocket-launchers to destroy enemy concrete beach fortifications. Pictured here is a wartime image of an M4 medium tank armed with the 7.2in Multiple Rocket Launcher M17. It was nicknamed the 'Whiz-bang' and saw use by the US army in both France and Italy. (*Patton Museum*)

Taking the concept of a specialized tank-based engineering vehicle one step further resulted in the US army building a single example of a pilot vehicle shown here labelled the T31 Demolition Tank. On either side of the strange-looking turret were T94 7.2inch Rocket Launchers. The barrel in the centre of the turret was a dummy. This vehicle was never ordered into production. *(TACOM)*

A very useful piece of engineering equipment mounted on the M4 series of medium tanks employed by the US army and USMC were bulldozer blade kits. Pictured here is a restored M4A3(105) tank fitted with the Bulldozer, Tank Mounting, M1, which had a 124in-wide blade. A total of 1,957 units of the M1 bulldozer blade were built during the Second World War. *(Pierre-Olivier Buan)*

Notes

Notes

Notes

Notes

Notes